꿣 Rice provides the chief source of food for half the world's population. Bland in flavor and non-allergenic, it combines equally well with meats, seafood, vegetables and dairy products to make some of the world's most memorable dishes . . . paella from Spain, calas from New Orleans, picadillo from Mexico, risottos from Italy, Chinese fried rice, Indian kitchree, Hungarian and Greek stuffed cabbage, rice a L'Imperatrice, and Puerto Rican black beans and rice are only a few.

꿣 There is no waste in rice. Every ounce is edible. There's no peeling or scraping . . . not even washing. It is easy to prepare because of its built-in convenience.

꿣 Rice which is an excellent extender of more expensive foods should save you money, not increase your food budget. This collection of recipes from around the world was put together with this in mind.

RICE

BETTY L. TORRE

CONDOR

NEW YORK

RICE

CONDOR

CONDOR edition published January 1978

ISBN 0-89516-017-X
Library of Congress Catalog Number: 77-83880

Printed in the United States of America

CONDOR PUBLISHING COMPANY, INC.
521 Fifth Avenue
New York, N.Y. 10017

Dedicated
to my husband Frank
and our two sons
Jason and Sean Patrick

CONTENTS

CONTENTS

AUTHOR'S NOTE

The recipes found in this cookbook have been the result of over ten years of looking for rice recipes to please my husband. Although the regular white Louisiana-type rice has been used when these recipes were tested at home, brown rice or other rices can be substituted by adjusting the cooking time and adding more liquid. In fact, half the fun of cooking rice is trying different rices.

INTRODUCTION

COOKING WITH RICE

Rice is probably our most versatile food. It provides the chief source of food for half the world's population. Bland in flavor and nonallergenic, it combines equally well with meats, seafood, vegetables and dairy products to make some of the world's most memorable dishes: paella from Spain, calas from New Orleans, picadillo from Mexico, risottos from Italy, Chinese fried rice, Indian kitchree, Greek rice soup, Puerto Rican black beans and rice, and rice à l'impératrice.

There is no waste in rice. Every particle is edible. What's more, there's no peeling or scraping. It comes ready to cook. Rice, because of its built-in convenience, is easy to prepare.

Recently in this country there has been a surge of interest in processed rices which are flavored with herbs and other seasonings. Unfortunately these additions—which can easily be prepared at home—increase the price of rice tremendously. Yet rice, which is an excellent extender of more expensive foods, should save you money, not increase your food budget. The following collection of recipes was put together with this in mind.

RICE: WHAT IS IT?

Rice is an annual cereal grass which originated in India and China. It was introduced into the West first by way of Egypt and then Greece, where it was already highly prized at the time of the philosopher Theophrastus (c.372–c.287 B.C.). Its popularity spread to Portugal, then to Italy and to America.

Its wild ancestor has been identified as *Oryza sativa*, a semiaquatic marsh grass native to India and southeast Asia. Most cultivated rice, known as aquatic rice, is grown in marshy or flooded lands, the sort of terrain found through much of the southern Orient and southeastern United States. It can also be grown, but with a lesser yield of lower quality, in areas where there is a long growing season and a great deal of steady rainfall. This type is called hill rice.

Rice yields more per acre than wheat or corn; and whereas wheat or barley must be ground first, rice can be eaten as a grain.

Rice is a highly nutritious and easily digested food. Almost all of it is completely assimilated. When milled so that only the husks are removed, producing "whole" or "brown" rice, eighty-eight percent of it consists of nutrients—about eight percent protein and seventy-nine percent carbohydrates (chiefly starch) with very small amounts of fat. The peoples who rely on rice as a mainstay of their diet always eat it in this state since further milling reduces its food value.

In modern processing, rice when harvested goes to a drying plant where hot air is blown through it to "cure" it and reduce its moisture content, assuring good keeping quality. The first step in the milling process is the removal of the husk, leaving what is sometimes called "natural brown rice." If the milling is carried further the next step involves the grinding away of several outer layers of the grain. This results in white rice. It also produces such by-products as rice bran and rice polishings, used mainly as stock feed.

In the next step all broken particles and any foreign seeds or defective grains are screened out, leaving clean white rice. The finer particles of broken rice are used in making beer. Larger broken particles are sometimes mixed with whole grains for extremely low cost table rice. Years ago, rice was given a coating of talc or glucose, which is why old recipes say "wash rice until the water runs clean." Nowadays this is not necessary. Rice no longer requires washing when it comes from a package.

BROWN RICE VERSUS WHITE RICE

Brown rice is rich in vitamins of the B complex, thiamine, niacin and riboflavin, and in iron and calcium. It is higher in many of these vitamins and minerals than enriched, parboiled or other processed rice. It also has a marvelous sweet and nutty flavor.

White rice is not, however, a scourge on humanity as some might have you believe. On the contrary, the discovery that refining rice would allow it to be stored for much longer periods without spoiling or becoming pest-infested has kept much of the world from starvation. Modern-day polished rice is also enriched with a few of the nutrients lost in processing.

With only its hull removed in milling, though, brown rice is clearly a nutritious product. The people who rely on rice for their principal nourishment always use it in its rough state, never polished.

TYPES OF RICE

The three most commonly used forms of rice in this country are brown, regular white and parboiled or converted rice.

Brown rice has only the hull removed and the bran coating remains on the grain, it requires more water when cooking and a longer cooking time. It is rich in vitamins of the B complex, thiamine, niacin and riboflavin, and in iron and calcium. It is higher in many of these vitamins and minerals than enriched, parboiled or other processed rice.

Regular white rice has the hull and bran layer removed as well as another coating when polished. It is marketed in short- and long-grain varieties. Each type has a specific purpose. Short-grain rice, the least expensive, cooks moist and is ideal for puddings, rice rings and casserole combinations. Long-grain rice cooks in less time and comes out fluffy with the grains separated. Most white rice today is lightly milled so that it retains its natural qualities.

Parboiled or converted rice is white rice that goes through special treatment. The grains are parboiled, strained and dried. The processing allows them to retain much of their vitamin B content. This type of rice is also treated to preserve food values that would otherwise get lost in polishing, and it's quick to prepare.

Among Americans the long-grain rice from Louisiana and Texas is probably the most popular, as it cooks into fluffy white grains; but the short-grain rice from California is extensively used for puddings and soups.

Rice is sold under various names, not always descriptive of its origin. The principal types are:

Carolina rice—Long-grained, angular, white or slightly bluish, bright and shiny.

Indo-Chinese rice—Smaller than Indian rice, it has excellent flavor and cooks perfectly without breaking up.

Java rice—Flat, transparent, shiny, with more elongated grains.

Patna rice—From India; less shiny, with grains softer and less transparent.

Basumati is a particular one.

Japanese rice—A glutinous type of rice shiny oval grains with a dark mark at the center; greyish-white. *Mochigome* is a particular one.

Roman rice—Greyish-white grains, dull.

Piedmont rice—Short rounded grains, very white and shiny, grayish and opaque in the center.

There are hundreds of rices, not counting wild rice, which isn't a rice at all, but a grass. Most rices may be cooked in the same way, but some require longer cooking time than others. Regular white rice was used in these recipes, so when you are using other varieties, start testing for tenderness sooner, and if necessary cook longer, adding more liquids.

How to Cook It

Cooking rice is an art that doesn't come easily to many of us. Overcooking, which reduces rice to a mush, has contributed to the disfavor in which this food has generally been held in the West. During the 1870–71 siege of Paris, when there was a shortage of bread, enormous quantities of rice remained unused.

However, you can learn to cook it so that each grain is separate and dry, yet tender, not gummy and sticky. There are several ways to accomplish this and good cooks have been known to come to blows over which way is the right one. All the peoples for whom rice is the staple diet are careful never to stir it while it is cooking, and never to cook it too long (twenty minutes on the average), so that the grains remain whole. Since each distributor knows his rice best, check instructions on the package that you buy.

Here are the basic methods used to cook rice.

Steaming: Add 1/2 teaspoon salt to 2 cups rapidly boiling water, then add 1 cup rice. Shake pot to level rice, cover, and reduce heat as low as possible. Cook (without removing cover) until rice is tender and all water absorbed. Regular white rice will take 18–20 minutes. Brown rice will take 40–45 minutes. If you like, uncover and let dry out for 3–5 minutes before serving. (Many Asians measure the amount of water with their index finger. Place finger on top of leveled rice. Water should come to the first joint.)

Boiling: Bring water and salt to a rapid boil over high heat in an extra heavy saucepan. Add rice, reduce heat slightly, and cook, uncovered, without stirring until water is barely visible, about 10 minutes. Turn heat to low and continue cooking, uncovered, until all moisture is absorbed, about 8–10 minutes. Fluff with a fork.

Baking: Preheat oven to 400° F. In a heavy flame-proof casserole, melt 2 tablespoons butter or margarine over direct moderate heat. Add rice and stir-fry for about 30 seconds. Add water and salt, cover tightly, and bake until rice is tender and all liquid absorbed. White rice will take 20–30 minutes; brown rice about 45 minutes. Fluff with a fork and serve.

TIPS FOR MAKING BETTER RICE

There are several *don'ts* to remember when cooking rice. *Don't* wash or rinse rice. You lose valuable vitamins and minerals. *Don't* peek when steaming rice, it lets out steam, lowers temperature. *Don't* stir rice after it comes to a boil. This mashes grains, makes rice gummy. *Don't* leave rice in the pan in which it was cooked for more than 5–10 minutes or cooked rice will pack.

Here are some *do's*:

—Be sure to use a large enough pan; rice will triple or quadruple in bulk during cooking. Also make sure the pan is heavy so there is little danger of scorching.

—Once rice comes to a boil, stir as little as possible, and use a fork if you must stir—there's less chance of mashing or breaking the rice.

—To help keep rice grains beautifully distinct, add 1 or 2 drops of cooking oil or a dab of butter or margarine to the cooking water. This also gives the rice a lovely glisten.

—If rice must be held before serving, transfer it to a colander and set it over simmering water; keep it covered. The rice will keep hot without overcooking. Alternatively, transfer it to a heavy casserole and set in an oven turned to its lowest heat. Keep tightly covered.

How to Test Rice for Tenderness

The easiest way is to taste it. Scoop out a few grains and bite into them. The grains should have no hardness in the center. As soon as the grains are tender all through but still firm, the rice is done.

How Much Rice Should You Cook

Since rice increases in bulk at least three times when cooked, allow one cup of rice for each three to six servings, depending upon whether it is as accompaniment to meats and vegetables or the basis of a one-dish meal.

1 cup regular white rice = 3 cups cooked rice

1 cup brown rice = 4 cups cooked rice

1 cup parboiled or converted rice = 4 cups cooked rice

Rice Measurements

A pound of rice measures 2 1/4 cups; 1 cup rice weighs about 6 3/4 ounces; 1/4 pound rice is a heaping 1/2 cup.

How Many Calories in Rice?

One serving of approximately 3 1/2 ounces of various cooked rices contains the following calories:

Brown rice = 119 calories

White rice = 109 calories

Parboiled or converted rice = 106 calories.

As you can see there is not an appreciable difference in the number of calories in each variety, but remember that, as with pasta, the foods which are eaten with rice bring the calorie count way up.

How to Store Rice

Store in a covered container in a cool, dry place. Uncooked rice will keep almost indefinitely.

Cooked rice is one of the few foods that can be refrigerated for about a week. When refrigerating rice, be sure to cover it so that the grains will not dry out or absorb the flavors of other foods.

How to Freeze Rice

Rice can be frozen with any food that will freeze. It can be kept in a frozen condition for about 6–8 months.

Some combination dishes that contain rice may appear dry when taken from the freezer. Add a little milk or water, about 1/3 cup, when reheating them.

Note. Do not overcook. Overcooking not only destroys the texture of foods, but it also gives them a warmed-over taste.

What to Do with Leftover Rice

To reheat: Place rice in a large, fine sieve and with moistened hands break up any clumps. Set the sieve over simmering water, cover, and steam for about 10 minutes. The rice will be almost as good as it was the first time around. A second method is to place the rice in a buttered casserole and break up clumps with moistened hands. Dot well with butter, cover, and bake 1/2 hour at 325° F.

To use up small amounts:
—Combine with leftover meat and vegetables in a casserole or soup.
—Mix into meat loaves, croquettes or stuffings.
—Add to any creamed meat or vegetable mixture.
—Marinate in garlic or herb dressing and serve in hollowed-out tomatoes.
—Toss with mixed greens in a salad.
—Add to pancake batter.
—Scramble with eggs.
—Team with custard sauce and/or fresh fruit as a dessert.

Equipment Needed

You won't need any special equipment when cooking rice recipes. The usual casseroles, skillets, saucepans, molds, measures, spoons, double boiler and strainer are all that will be necessary.

Electric rice cookers turn out quite acceptable rice. Most are made in the Orient. They are easy to operate and wholly automatic—you just add the rice and water. Cooking time is about 20 minutes. If you have everything else you want in your kitchen, you might think of buying one.

Rice
In
Soups

AVGOLEMONO SOUP

Greek Egg and Lemon Soup

Preparation and Cooking Time: 30 minutes   Serves 4

One of the truly great, simple soups of the world.

INGREDIENTS
1 quart chicken stock
1/4 cup rice

2 eggs
Juice of 1 lemon
Minced fresh parsley

DIRECTIONS
Bring broth to a boil; add rice and cook until rice is tender, about 20 minutes. Lower heat.

Beat eggs until light and foamy. Add lemon juice and beat again. Add a cup of hot soup and beat until well blended. Add egg-and-lemon mixture to the rest of the soup, stirring constantly. Heat almost to the boiling point, but not quite or the soup will curdle. Serve immediately, sprinkled with minced fresh parsley.

VARIATION
Substitute port wine for lemon juice and you have Portuguese rice soup.

ITALIAN RICE SOUP WITH LEMON

Preparation and Cooking Time: 20 minutes   Serves 4–6

A thinner soup can be made by using more stock.

INGREDIENTS
½ cup uncooked rice
6 cups chicken or beef stock

DIRECTIONS
Add rice to boiling chicken or beef stock. Boil it until rice is cooked to taste, about 20 minutes.

2 egg yolks,
Juice of ½ lemon
¼ cup freshly grated Parmesan cheese
2 tablespoons water

Beat together egg yolks, lemon juice, grated cheese and water. Pour this mixture into a soup, stirring constantly.

RAISIN AND RICE SOUP

Preparation and Cooking Time: 3 hours **Serves 4**

An unusual, sweet soup which is not for everyone.

INGREDIENTS	DIRECTIONS
1/4 cup raisins 1/4 cup sherry, warmed 1/4 cup warm water	Soak raisins in warm water and sherry for 1 hour.
1 cup fresh peas or frozen peas, thawed 1 cup small green beans, cut into 1-inch pieces 3 tablespoons butter 1½ quarts boiling water Salt to taste	Prepare vegetables. Heat butter in a saucepan; add peas and beans and stir-fry for 1 minute. Add the boiling water and season with salt. Cover and simmer very gently for 2½ hours.
1 cup cooked rice	Add rice and raisins with liquid; cook 20 minutes longer. Adjust seasoning and serve hot.

CHINESE RICE CRUST OR CAKE

Rice cake or crust is the firm, crisp mass that forms when ordinary rice is left over low heat for an hour or so after most of the rice has been removed from the pot. The "overcooked" rice on the bottom takes on a golden color and a nutty flavor. This cake or crust can be deep-fried. Soup is often poured on the fried rice crust or cake at the table, making it sizzle or sing dramatically. Try it with egg drop soup.

EGG DROP SOUP

Preparation and Cooking Time: 10 minutes   **Serves 4**

Egg drop soup is a great Western favorite. Serve it over Chinese rice crust or cake for a change.

INGREDIENTS
1 quart chicken broth
¼ cup cornstarch
Salt to taste

DIRECTIONS
Blend a little chicken broth with the cornstarch. Bring the rest of the chicken broth to a boil; season with salt to taste. Stir in cornstarch mixture. When soup has thickened and cooked for 1 minute, turn off heat.

1 egg, well beaten

Add egg in a thin stream, stirring constantly in a circular fashion so that egg forms thin shreds in the hot broth.

Fried rice crust or cake
1 scallion with green top, chopped

Pour over fried rice crust or cake in individual bowls.
Sprinkle with scallion. Serve hot.

*Does not include time to make rice crust and to fry it.

LENTILS WITH RICE

Preparation and Cooking Time: 1 hour 30 minutes **Serves 4**

Italians consider this dish a soup and serve it as a first course.

INGREDIENTS

1½ quarts water
Pinch of salt
1 cup dry lentils, cleaned and washed

2 tablespoons olive oil
1 garlic clove, halved
1 8-ounce can tomato sauce

½ teaspoon salt
⅛ teaspoon freshly ground black pepper
½ teaspoon basil

3 cups not cooked rice

DIRECTIONS

Bring salted water to a boil in a small pot; add lentils and simmer for 1 hour or unitl tender. Drain when cooked.

When lentils are almost cooked, heat olive oil in a large saucepan; sauté garlic until limp but not brown. Add tomato sauce and simmer for 10 minutes.

Add drained lentils, salt, black pepper, and basil to sauce; cook over low heat for 15 minutes more.

Add drained rice and let sit 5 minutes on turned-off burner before serving.

VARIATION

Use dried white beans instead of lentils. Beans will take longer to cook.

MINESTRONE

Italian Vegetable Soup

Preparation and Cooking Time: 1 hour 30 minutes

Serves 4–6

Who can resist Italy's most famous soup?

INGREDIENTS
1/2 pound salt pork, chopped

1 medium onion, chopped
1 small garlic clove, minced
1 tablespoon minced fresh parsley
1 teaspoon salt
1/4 teaspoon freshly ground black pepper.

1 tablespoon tomato paste
1 cup water

1 cup chopped celery
3 carrots, sliced
2 potatoes, peeled and diced
2 cups canned pea beans
1 1/2 cups shredded cabbage

DIRECTIONS
Sauté diced salt pork for 5 minutes.

Add onions, garlic, parsley, salt and pepper. Cook for 10 minutes over low heat.

Add tomato paste and water; bring to a boil and cook for 5 minutes.

Add all the vegetables and broth. Bring to a boil and cook over low heat for 1 hour.

½ pound zucchini, diced
1 cup peas
1½ quarts beef broth
   or water

3 cups cooked rice	Add rice and cook for 5 minutes more. Adjust seasoning if necessary.
Freshly grated Parmesan cheese	Serve with grated cheese.

SOUTH AMERICAN VEGETABLE SOUP

Preparation and Cooking Time: 2 hours   **Serves 4–6**

Chicken, potatoes and squash form the basis for this lovely soup.

INGREDIENTS	DIRECTIONS
1 3-pound stewing chicken, cut up Water to cover	Place chicken in an enamel soup pot with enough water to cover it. Stew until tender, about 1 hour. Remove chicken from broth. Reserve broth.
3 tablespoons butter 1 large onion, sliced 2 large potatoes, peeled and diced	Brown chicken pieces in butter with onions and potatoes. Put mixture into soup pot.
½ pound squash, peeled and cubed	Add squash, string beans, rice, salt and crushed red

9

1 cup string beans,
   cleaned and broken
   into 1-inch lengths
1½ tablespoons rice
Salt to taste
Pinch of crushed red
pepper

pepper. Simmer until the
vegetables are tender.

1 egg yolk
2 tablespoons fresh
   minced parsley

Stir in egg yolk and gar-
nish with chopped pars-
ley before serving.

SPANISH VEGETABLE SOUP WITH RICE

Preparation and Cooking Time: 2 hours 30 minutes

Serves 4–6

Both, pasta and rice are added to this soup filled with
potatoes, turnips, beans and cabbage.

INGREDIENTS
1 3-pound stewing
   chicken, cut in half
3 quarts water
1 tablespoon salt

DIRECTIONS
Place chicken and water
in a large enamel soup
pot; bring to a full boil,
and boil for 10 minutes.
Remove from heat and
skim off black scum
which gathers on top of
broth.

Add salt and simmer 1½
hours. Remove chicken
from stock and use in an-
other dish. Strain stock
for a clearer soup.

2 medium potatoes,
  peeled and diced
2 medium white turnips,
  peeled and diced
1/2 cup cooked kidney
  beans
1 cup chopped cabbage
1 stalk of celery with
  leaves, chopped

Cook vegetables in the stock until tender.

1/4 cup uncooked rice
1/2 cup vermicelli, broken
  into 1-inch lengths
Salt to taste
Pinch of saffron

Add the rice, vermicelli, salt and saffron and cook for 20 minutes longer.

VARIATION
Use veal stock instead of chicken stock.
Shred chicken and return to soup for a heartier dish.

MULLIGATAWNY SOUP

Preparation and Cooking Time: 1 hour 30 minutes **Serves 4**

The juice of a lime is added to the soup just before serving for an unusual touch.

INGREDIENTS
1/4 cup diced salt pork

DIRECTIONS
Fry salt pork until rendered of its fat.

1 carrot, chopped
3 medium onions, sliced
1 small turnip, chopped

Add carrot, onions and turnip; cook for 3 minutes with the salt

11

pork, stirring occasionally.

2 tablespoons curry powder Pinch of cayenne pepper 1/4 cup flour Salt to taste	Sprinkle with curry powder, cayenne and flour; blend well. Cook until onion is limp and golden. Season with salt.
1 tablespoon chopped fresh parsley 1 garlic clove, minced 1 stalk rhubarb, chopped 1 quart of chicken stock	Add parsley, garlic, rhubarb and stock; bring to a boil. Lower heat and simmer very slowly 1 hour.
Juice of 1 lime 3 cups hot cooked rice	Just before serving, skim soup and add lime juice. This is served with rice passed separately.

PEA AND RICE SOUP

Preparation and Cooking Time: 1 hour 30 minutes

Serves 4–6

The peas and rice in this hearty, savory soup should be al dente—not mushy.

INGREDIENTS	DIRECTIONS
1 pound (about 2 cups) dried split peas, cleaned and washed 2 1/2 quarts cold water	Place washed peas in cold water in a large enamel soup pot; bring to a full boil before lowering heat so soup can simmer.
1/4 pound slab bacon, cubed	Fry bacon for 5 minutes or until almost done;

2 medium onions, sliced	then add onion and sauté in bacon fat until limp and golden; add mixture to pea soup.
1 teaspoon salt ¼ teaspoon freshly ground black pepper	Season with salt and black pepper. Simmer soup until peas are tender, about 45–60 minutes.
3 cups hot cooked rice	Add rice to finished soup; allow to sit 5 minutes before serving.

RISI E BISI

Preparation and Cooking Time: 30 minutes   **Serves 4**

This famous Venetian dish is considered by Italians to be a soup, but it is usually even thicker than most Italian soups.

INGREDIENTS
3 tablespoons butter
2 slices prosciutto ham or bacon, minced fine
1 scallion with green top, finely chopped
1 medium stalk of celery with leaves, finely chopped

DIRECTIONS
Melt butter in a large saucepan; add prosciutto, scallion and celery, and sauté until vegetables are limp. (This type of sautéed mixture is called *soffritto* or *battuto* in Italian.)

1 cup uncooked rice
2 cups fresh peas or 1 package frozen peas, thawed and drained
3½ cups hot chicken stock
½ teaspoon salt

Add rice and stir constantly until translucent; then add peas for a moment until well coated. Pour in stock; season with salt and pepper.

13

Pinch of freshly ground black pepper	Bring to a boil; lower heat and simmer covered until stock is almost absorbed, about 20 minutes. Stir occasionally.
1 tablespoon butter **1 tablespoon freshly grated Parmesan cheese**	Stir in butter and grated cheese. Serve with additional cheese.

VARIATIONS
The combination of rice and peas is traditional, but other vegetables such as string beans, mushrooms or sliced zucchini can be substituted.

SPINACH AND RICE SOUP

Preparation and Cooking Time: 30 minutes   **Serves 4**

A refreshing, light soup.

INGREDIENTS
1 medium onion, chopped
2 tablespoons butter

DIRECTIONS
Sauté onions in butter in a large saucepan until limp and golden.

4 cups chicken broth
1/4 cup uncooked rice

Add broth and bring to a boil.

1 package chopped frozen spinach, thawed
1 teaspoon salt
Pinch of nutmeg
Pinch of freshly ground

Stir in rice and simmer rapidly, uncovered, for 10 minutes until rice is about half done. Add spinach, salt, nutmeg and black pepper

black pepper. Simmer 10 minutes longer or until rice is tender. Adjust seasoning if necessary.

TOMATO SOUP

Preparation and Cooking Time: 30 minutes   **Serves 4**

Flavored with onion and green pepper.

INGREDIENTS
1 medium onion, chopped
1 small green pepper, cored, seeded and chopped
3 tablespoons olive oil
4 medium fresh tomatoes, peeled and diced
½ cup uncooked rice

1½ quarts water
Salt and freshly ground black pepper to taste
¼ cup chopped fresh parsley

DIRECTIONS
Sauté onion and pepper in olive oil until onion is limp and golden.

Add tomatoes and rice and continue to sauté for 5 minutes.

Add water, salt and pepper, and parsley. Bring to a boil; lower heat and simmer until rice is tender, about 20 minutes.

ANCHOVY AND RICE SOUP

Preparation and Cooking Time: 40 minutes   **Serves 4**

A soup with an unusual flavor.

INGREDIENTS
4 tablespoons butter
I medium onion, minced

1/3 cup uncooked rice
I small tin anchovy fillets,
  smashed
I quart beef stock

Freshly grated Parmesan
  cheese

DIRECTIONS
Sauté onion in butter in a
saucepan until onion is
limp and golden.

Add rice and anchovies;
sauté until rice is golden.
Add beef stock; simmer,
covered, for 30 minutes.

Serve hot with grated
cheese.

SALMON AND RICE SOUP

Preparation and Cooking Time: 20 minutes   **Serves 4**

A rich, creamy soup.

INGREDIENTS
1 tablespoon butter
1 small onion, minced

DIRECTIONS
Heat butter in a saucepan; sauté onion until limp and golden. Push onion to one side of pan.

3 tablespoons butter
3 tablespoons flour
3 cups fish or chicken stock

Melt butter in pan; then stir in flour until smooth. Add stock, stirring constantly, until thickened.

1/4 cup cream
Salt and freshly ground
    black pepper to taste

Add cream and season with salt and black pepper to taste. Simmer for a few minutes.

1 7-ounce can salmon,
    skinned and boned

Add half of the salmon. Remove from heat and cool slightly. Then purée the soup in a blender until smooth.

1/4 cup dry white wine
Juice of 1/2 lemon

Add wine, lemon juice, and the rest of the salmon to soup and blend for a second or two more. Soup should have a slightly coarse consistency.

| ½ cup cooked rice | Add rice; return to pan and reheat, but do not boil. |
| Toasted bread croutons
1 tablespoon minced fresh parsley | Serve with croutons and minced parsley on top. |

GREEK EGG-LEMON SOUP WITH MEATBALLS

Preparation and Cooking Time: 45 minutes   **Serves 4–6**

My friend Mrs. Joe (Chris) LaRosa serves this hearty soup as a complete meal with Italian or French bread.

INGREDIENTS

2 quarts canned chicken broth

Salt and freshly ground black pepper to taste

To make meatballs:
1 pound ground beef
¼ cup uncooked white rice
3 tablespoons minced fresh mint or 1½ tablespoons dried mint
1 teaspoon salt
¼ teaspoon freshly ground black pepper

DIRECTIONS

Heat chicken broth while you make the meatballs. Season to taste.

Mix together in a large bowl the ground beef, rice, mint, salt and black pepper. Wet hands in cold water before forming meat mixture into round balls, about the size of a walnut. Handle meat mixture gently. *Do not pack meatballs.* Add meatballs to hot broth and cook 30 minutes.

To make sauce:
2 large eggs, well beaten
Juice of a lemon
or 2 ounces lemon juice

When ready to serve, beat eggs in a 4-cup measuring cup (this makes it easy to pour later on) or a large bowl. Add lemon juice.

Slowly stir some of the hot broth into eggs. Continue to beat while adding more broth until cup is full. Stir egg-lemon mixture into soup; continue to mix so eggs won't curdle. Remove from heat. Serve at once.

VARIATIONS
Without the meatballs, this is Greek egg-lemon soup. You can also cook manestra (a type of pasta) in broth before adding the egg-lemon mixture.

CONGEE (JOOK)

Preparation and Cooking Time: 2 hours   **Serves 4**

The Cantonese call this rice soup **jook** and the English-speaking people in the Orient call it **congee**. It is nothing more than rice cooked in much more liquid than usual.

INGREDIENTS
1½ quarts fish or chicken
    stock
½ cup uncooked rice

DIRECTIONS
Put stock into a soup pot and bring to a vigorous boil. Add rice and bring to a boil again. Simmer, covered, for 2 hours or until grains of rice disintegrate.

VARIATIONS
Any meat, except raw pork, can be sliced thin, mairnated, and added to this dish. All seafood, such as shrimp, oysters, fish filets, can be prepared and used in this way. The heat of the jook will cook the meat or seafood. Roast pork is a delicious addition.

Just bring jook base to a vigorous boil. Ladle it on top of the marinated meat or seafood in soup bowls. Let stand for 5 minutes, stir jook gently, top with chopped scallions and serve.

To make marinade:
1½ tablespoons soy sauce
1 tablespoon oil
½ teaspoon sugar
Pinch of salt and white pepper
1 teaspoon sherry (optional)
1 slice of fresh ginger (optional)
This is enough marinade for 1 cup thinly sliced steak, chicken breast, fish fillets or other seafood. Marinate for 1 hour.

LAMB SOUP WITH RICE

Preparation and Cooking Time: 3 hours   Serves 4–6

A hearty soup filled with rice and lentils.

INGREDIENTS	DIRECTIONS
1 pound cubed lamb	Brown lamb in its own fat.
5 cups water Salt and freshly ground black pepper to taste	Add water, salt and pepper; bring to a boil, reduce heat and simmer, covered, for 2½ hours.
1 cup lentils, washed	Add to lamb and cook 15 minutes.

21

1 tablespoon butter 1 large onion, chopped	Brown onion in butter and then add to soup.
1 cup uncooked rice	Add rice; cover and continue cooking until rice and lentils are tender, stirring occasionally. The soup should be thick.

Basic
Side
Dishes

❧

STEAMED RICE

Preparation and Cooking Time: 20 minutes   Serves 4-6

Many Asians measure amount of the stock by putting their index finger on top of rice. Liquid should come to first joint.

INGREDIENTS
2 cups cold water or stock
1 cup uncooked rice
1 teaspoon salt

DIRECTIONS
Put rice, water or stock, and salt in a heavy saucepan with a tight-fitting cover. (Reduce salt if stock is used.) Bring to a boil; reduce heat and simmer, covered for 15 minutes without removing lid or stirring.

VARIATION
Toss with butter and toasted almonds when cooked.

Mix steamed rice cooked in stock with mushrooms sautéed in butter.

Add ⅛ teaspoon powdered saffron to cooking liquid. Season to taste with salt and black pepper.

Add 2 tablespoons poppy or caraway seeds and melted butter. Season to taste with salt and black pepper.

Add ⅛ cup minced pitted olives and 2 tablespoons olive oil. Season to taste.

Add 1 coarsely chopped small avocado and ½ cup coarsely chopped, peeled and seeded tomato. Season to taste.

Add ¼ cup minced fresh mint warmed for 3 minutes in 2 tablespoons butter. Season to taste.

Add 1 cup sour cream. Sprinkle with 2 tablespoons minced chives.

½ cup freshly grated cheddar, Parmesan or mozzarella cheese.

BASIC WILD RICE

Preparation and Cooking Time: 50 minutes   **Serves 6**

Especially good with game or poultry.

INGREDIENTS
¾ cup wild rice
3 cups water
1 teaspoon salt

DIRECTIONS
Combine wild rice, water and salt in a large saucepan; bring to a boil.
Cover and simmer for about 45 minutes or until tender.

2 tablespoons butter, at
..room temperature

Mix with butter.

VARIATIONS
Mix wild rice with sautéed mushrooms.

Mix wild rice with ¼ cup minced cooked ham or bacon bits.

BASIC BROWN RICE

Preparation and Cooking Time: 50 minutes   **Serves 4–6**

Adds a nutlike texture. High in nutrients.

INGREDIENTS
1 cup uncooked brown rice
2 tablespoons oil

DIRECTIONS
Put rice and oil in a skillet; cook, stirring constantly, over low heat for 5 minutes until rice is light brown.

4 cups water
1 teaspoon salt

Add water and salt; bring to a boil. Cover and cook for about 45 minutes on low heat or until all water is absorbed.

VARIATIONS
Proceed to vary as you would with any white rice.

BASIC RICE PILAF

Preparation and Cooking Time: 30 minutes   **Serves 4**

INGREDIENTS
1/4 cup butter or margarine
1 cup uncooked rice
2 cups hot chicken or beef

DIRECTIONS
Melt butter in a heavy saucepan over moderate heat; add rice and stir-fry

broth
½ teaspoon salt
⅛ teaspoon freshly ground
    black pepper

for about 5 minutes until translucent. (*Note.* "Stir-fry" means fry quickly in hot oil or butter while stirring constantly.)

Add broth, salt and pepper; cover and cook over lowest heat, without stirring, for 18–20 minutes until all liquid is absorbed. Uncover and cook 3–5 minutes longer to dry out. Fluff with a fork and readjust seasoning.

VARIATIONS

Baked Pilaf

Stir-fry rice as directed in a Dutch oven; add broth and seasonings. Cover and bake for about 30 minutes at 350° F. until all liquid is absorbed. For a drier rice, uncover and bake for 5 minutes longer.

Baked pilaf is a good way to make pilaf in a large quantity.

RISOTTO ALLA MILANESE

Preparation and Cooking Time: 30 minutes   **Serves 4**

There are dozens of risotti (soft rice mixtures that are to the north of Italy what pasta is to the south). This one is a classic. Delicious with veal or chicken.

INGREDIENTS
2 tablespoons butter
2 tablespoons olive oil
1 small onion, chopped fine
1 small garlic, chopped fine

1 cup uncooked rice
1/2 cup dry white wine
3 cups hot chicken stock,
  approximately

Pinch of powdered saffron
1 tablespoon freshly grated
  Parmesan cheese
1 tablespoon butter
1/2 teaspoon salt
Pinch of freshly ground
  black pepper

DIRECTIONS
Heat butter and olive oil in a large skillet; sauté onion and garlic until onion is limp and golden.

Add rice and stir until translucent. Pour in wine and cook until almost evaporated; then add 1 cup hot stock; cook over moderate heat, stirring frequently. Add more stock as previous addition is absorbed. Toward end of cooking, stir continually with a two-pronged fork to avoid sticking.

Dissolve saffron in a little stock; add to pan with grated cheese, butter, salt and black pepper. Stop adding more stock when rice is tender with still a little "bite" to each grain.

VARIATIONS

Sauté a sliced zucchini with the onion and garlic. Proceed as directed above.

Mushroom Risotto

Stir-fry ½ pound minced mushrooms along with onion and rice. Proceed as directed. Toss ¼ cup piñon nuts with cheese.

Savory Risotto

Omit onion, but stir-fry rice, adding 1 minced garlic clove during last minutes. Add 1 cup each white wine and chicken broth, seasonings and proceed.

Chicken Liver Risotto

Sauté 1 pound chicken livers. Add onions and mushrooms. Proceed as directed.

SOY SAUCE RICE SNACK

Preparation and Cooking Time: 2 minutes   **Serves 4**

A simple, unassuming dish made with leftover rice. Chinese children eat this as a snack after school. The rice, which should be at room temperature rather than cold, is mixed with oil and sprinkled with dark soy sauce and finely chopped scallions.

INGREDIENTS
- 3 cups cooked rice, at room temperature
- 2 tablespoons peanut oil
- 3 tablespoons dark soy sauce
- 2 scallions with green tops, finely chopped

DIRECTIONS
Add oil to rice and mix thoroughly. Then add soy sauce and mix again. The oil must be put in and mixed first so that each grain is coated and the soy sauce will distribute evenly. Sprinkle with chopped scallions and mix again.

BASIC FRIED RICE

Preparation and Cooking Time: 15 minutes   **Serves 4**

Fried rice is an excellent way to use leftover cooked rice as well as leftover vegetables, bits of meat and poultry.

INGREDIENTS
- 1 tablespoon oil
- ½ cup coarsely chopped bamboo shoots

DIRECTIONS
Sauté bamboo shoots, mushrooms and scallions in hot oil in a large skillet

½ cup coarsely chopped
    fresh mushrooms
2 scallions with tops,
    chopped

for about 5 minutes.

3 cups cooked rice
1 cup cooked diced pork
    or chicken

Stir in rice and diced pork. Cook over low heat, stirring constantly.

½ cup fish or chicken
    broth
2 teaspoons soy sauce

Add broth and soy sauce. Continue cooking over low heat, stirring constantly, until liquid is absorbed.

JAPANESE FRIED RICE

Preparation and Cooking Time. 15 minutes   **Serves 4**

To make fried rice successfully, use rice which has been stored overnight in the refrigerator. This will prevent the rice from becoming sticky when fried.

INGREDIENTS
2 tablespoons oil
1 egg, beaten

DIRECTIONS
Heat oil in a skillet; add egg and scramble briefly.

3 cups cooked rice
4 chopped scallions with
    tops
½ cup cooked shrimp,
    crabmeat, diced pork
    or ham
½ cup cooked green peas

Add rice, scallions, seafood and green peas. Cook over medium heat for 5 minutes, stirring gently.

1 tablespoon soy sauce	Add soy sauce; mix thoroughly before serving.

PORK FRIED RICE

Preparation and Cooking Time: 30 minutes   **Serves 4**

This is probably the most popular Chinese dish in this country, and an excellent way of using up leftovers. All ingredients must be prepared before beginning to cook Chinese dishes.

INGREDIENTS	DIRECTIONS
2 tablespoons oil 1/2 small onion, diced 1 garlic clove, minced 1 teaspoon salt	Heat oil in a large skillet. Add onion and garlic; sprinkle with salt, and cook, stirring occasionally, until limp and golden.
1/3 cup sliced fresh mushrooms 1/2 cup sliced water chestnuts 1/3 cup frozen peas, thawed and drained	When skillet is sizzling hot, stir-fry mushrooms, chestnuts and peas for 2 minutes.
4 cups cooked chilled rice	Add rice and stir-fry for 2 minutes more until hot and well mixed with vegetables.
1/2 cup shredded cooked pork 1/8 teaspoon freshly ground black pepper 1/2 teaspoon sugar	Toss pork, black pepper and sugar together with rice mixture.

2 tablespoons soy sauce	Add soy sauce to skillet; stir-fry for 3 minutes.
1 tablespoon oil 2 eggs, beaten	Move rice to one side of pan; add oil and then beaten eggs. Allow eggs to begin to set before blending with rice mixture.
1 scallion with green top, chopped fine	Add chopped scallion and stir for 1 minute more. Serve at once.

VARIATIONS
Substitute cooked shrimp or chicken for pork.

GREEK PILAF

Preparation and Cooking Time: 30 minutes   Serves 4-6

A basic recipe which can be expanded as you wish.

INGREDIENTS	DIRECTIONS
6 tablespoons butter 1 cup uncooked rice 1/2 cup finely chopped onion	Melt butter in a heavy casserole. Add rice and onion, sauté until onion is limp and golden.
2 1/4 cups boiling chicken stock	Add boiling stock and season to taste. Cover and simmer for 20 minutes without stirring.

VARIATION
Add ½ cup tomato sauce to stock if a tomato flavor is desired. Onion may be omitted.

GOHAN

Japanese Steamed Rice

Preparation and Cooking Time: 1 hour　　　　Serves 4

Japanese rice is sticky, not in separate grains, to make it easier to pick up with chopsticks.

INGREDIENTS
1 cup uncooked rice
1½ cups cold water
½ teaspoon salt

DIRECTIONS
Put rice, water and salt in a saucepan and let soak for 30 minutes. Then bring to a boil; cover and cook over medium heat for 10 minutes. Turn heat down as low as possible and cook for 5 minutes more.

Turn off heat and let stand for 10 minutes more.

To reheat leftover rice, place in a colander over boiilng water. Cover and steam for 5 minutes.

INDIAN RICE WITH BUTTERMILK

Preparation Time: 5 minutes*   **Serves 4**

A cold rice which is made in India for picnics.

INGREDIENTS
1½ cups cold cooked rice
1 cup buttermilk
1 large garlic clove,
   minced
1 teaspoon minced hot
   green chili pepper
¼ cup chopped fresh
   coriander
Salt to taste

DIRECTIONS
Combine ingredients in a bowl. Add more buttermilk if rice does not hold together. Press into a pan; chill. Cut into squares and serve cold.

*Does not include chilling time.

CHESTNUT RICE

Preparation and Cooking Time: 40 minutes   **Serves 4–6**

A Japanese dish flavored with sake and soy sauce.

INGREDIENTS
12 chestnuts
Water to cover

DIRECTIONS
Cut a gash in each chestnut. Bring water to boil; boil chestnuts for 5 minutes. Drain and peel chestnuts while hot. Slice each one in half.

37

2 cups uncooked rice, washed
3 cups water
1 tablespoon soy sauce
1 tablespoon sake
1/4 teaspoon salt

Put rice, water, chestnuts, soy sauce, sake and salt in a covered pan. Bring to a rolling boil; reduce heat and cook for 20 minutes. Remove from heat and allow to stand undisturbed for 10 minutes before removing cover.

AFRICAN COCONUT RICE

Preparation and Cooking Time: 1 hour   Serves 4–6

Rice is cooked in coconut milk as is sometimes done in the Far East. The West African touch is the addition of tomatoes and onions.

INGREDIENTS
Meat from 1 fresh coconut, grated
2 1/2 cups water

DIRECTIONS
Cover grated coconut with water. Let soak 20–30 minutes. Place in colander and drain over a bowl, squeezing out as much liquid as possible. You should have about 2 cups coconut milk. If not, add a bit more water to the grated coconut and drain again. Bring coconut milk to a boil.

1 teaspoon dried ground crayfish, or to taste
1 cup rice

Add ground dried crayfish and rice; cover, reduce heat, and simmer

38

until rice is almost cooked.

2 cups canned tomatoes, undrained 1 small onion, chopped Salt to taste Cayenne pepper to taste	Stir in tomatoes, onion, salt and cayenne. Cook until water is completely absorbed and rice is quite dry.

HASHED BROWN RICE

Preparation and Cooking Time: 25 minutes **Serves 4**

This is as good as it is fast and easy to make. A crispy brown dish to serve with steak.

INGREDIENTS	DIRECTIONS
3 cups cooked rice 3 tablespoons flour 1/4 cup milk	Combine rice, flour and milk. Set aside.
2 tablespoons butter or margarine 1/2 cup chopped onion	Sauté onion in butter until tender in a large skillet. Mix with rice mixture.
Salt and freshly ground black pepper to taste	Add salt and pepper to taste. Spread rice mixture evenly in a greased skillet; press down firmly. Cook over medium heat until bottom is golden brown. Turn out onto serving dish, brown side up. Serve immediately.

39

MEXICAN RICE

Preparation and Cooking Time: 45 minutes   **Serves 4**

A spicy rice to serve with meatloaf or hamburgers.

INGREDIENTS
2 tablespoons olive oil
1 cup uncooked rice

1 small onion, minced
½ cup green peppers, chopped
2 teaspoons salt
2 teaspoons chili powder, or to taste
1 cup canned tomatoes, undrained
2 cups water

DIRECTIONS
Brown rice in hot oil in a large skillet until translucent.

Add onion, green pepper, salt, chili powder and tomatoes; mix well with water; cover and allow to simmer until rice is tender, about 30 minutes. Remove lid and allow mixture to dry out.

ORANGE RICE

Preparation and Cooking Time: 30 minutes   **Serves 4–6**

Agreeably pungent, orange rice is a perfect accompaniment for duck or other poultry.

INGREDIENTS
3 tablespoons butter or margarine
⅔ cup sliced celery

DIRECTIONS
Sauté celery and onion in melted butter until tender in a saucepan.

2 **tablespoons chopped onion**

1½ cups water	Stir in water, orange
1 cup orange juice	juice, orange peel and
2 tablespoons grated orange peel	salt; bring to a boil.
1¼ teaspoons salt	

1 cup uncooked rice	Add rice, cover, and steam over low heat 20 minutes or until rice is tender. Do not remove cover during cooking period.

PACHA RICE

Preparation and Cooking Time: 45 minutes   **Serves 4**

An excellent rice and vermicelli dish from Egypt, to serve with lamb kebabs or use as a poultry stuffing.

INGREDIENTS

DIRECTIONS

⅓ cup chopped, peeled almonds (or your favorite nuts)	Prepare almonds and raisins. Reserve.
⅓ cup raisins, soaked in hot water	

3 tablespoons butter	Heat butter in a large
1 medium onion, finely chopped	skillet; sauté onion and chicken livers until onion
½ pound finely chopped chicken livers	is limp and golden and chicken livers are lightly browned.

41

1 garlic clove, minced
1/8 teaspoon saffron
Pinch of thyme
Pinch of coriander
Pinch of basil
Pinch of cayenne pepper
Salt and freshly ground
  black pepper to taste
1 cup rice
Water

Add garlic, saffron, thyme, coriander, basil and cayenne pepper. Stir in nuts, well-drained raisins and rice. Add enough water to cover mixture by ½ inch (about 2 cups). Bring to a boil; reduce heat and cook rice in a covered pan for 16 minutes. Rice will be yellow and shiny when done.

1/4 pound vermicelli,
  broken into 1-inch
  lengths
Boiling water

Cook vermicelli in boiling water for 3 minutes. Drain and run cold water over it. Drain thoroughly.

1 tablespoon oil

Heat oil in another skillet; sauté well-drained vermicelli for 5 minutes, turning gently. When rice is done, stir in the vermicelli. Cook for 5 minutes more over low heat to blend flavors.

PEANUT RICE

Preparation and Cooking Time: 10 minutes   **Serves 4**

Delicious with chicken or ham.

INGREDIENTS	DIRECTIONS
2 cups cooked rice 1 cup finely chopped celery 1/2 cup finely chopped salted peanuts	Mix together rice, celery and salted peanuts. Cover and cook over low heat for 10 minutes to heat through.

PONGAL

Indian Rice

Preparation and Cooking Time: 45 minutes   **Serves 4-6**

This rice dish has the same name as the January harvest festival in South India.

INGREDIENTS	DIRECTIONS
1/2 cup green split peas 2 tablespoons butter	Fry peas in butter, in a skillet until lightly browned.
3 1/2 cups water 3/4 cup uncooked rice	Add water and bring to a boil. Add rice and cook until very soft.

2/3 cup sugar 2 tablespoons water	In a separate saucepan boil sugar add water to a syrup, about 10 minutes. Add to rice and bean mixture when cooked.
1/2 cup cashew nuts 1/2 cup raisins	Stir in nuts, raisins and butter.
4 tablespoons butter Pinch of ground cloves Pinch of cardamon	Serve hot sprinkled with cloves and cardamon.

SAFFRON RICE

Preparation and Cooking Time: 30 minutes   **Serves 4**

Saffron rice should have a fairly dry consistency.

INGREDIENTS	DIRECTIONS
2 tablespoons butter 1 cup uncooked rice 2 shallots, minced	Melt butter in a large saucepan; sauté rice and shallots until rice is transparent.
3½ cups chicken stock ½ teaspoon saffron Salt and freshly ground black pepper to taste	Add stock and bring to a boil. Lower heat and season with saffron, salt and black pepper. Cover and simmer until rice is tender, about 20 minutes.

44

SALAMI RISOTTO

Preparation and Cooking Time: 30 minutes   **Serves 4**

A basic risotto flavored with salami.

INGREDIENTS	DIRECTIONS
2 tablespoons butter 2 tablespoons olive oil I small onion, diced I garlic clove, minced	Sauté onion and garlic in olive oil and butter in a large skillet until limp and golden.
I cup uncooked rice	Stir in rice until golden.
I cup hot chicken stock	Add stock, cover, and simmer until almost absorbed, about 5 minutes.
2¼ cups hot chicken stock 3 tablespoons tomato sauce	Add rest of stock and tomato sauce; cover and simmer for 10 minutes more or until rice is tender.
½ cup Italian salami, sliced rather thick and cubed ¼ cup freshly grated Parmesan cheese I tablespoon butter	When rice is done, stir in salami, cheese and butter; let sit for 3 minutes before serving to allow flavors to blend.

SPANISH RICE

Preparation and Cooking Time: 20 minutes   **Serves 4–6**

Highly seasoned rice topped with cheddar cheese is an excellent accompaniment for steak or hamburgers.

INGREDIENTS
3 slices bacon, chopped

DIRECTIONS
Fry bacon in a large saucepan until crisp. Remove bacon from pan; pour off drippings, leaving 1 tablespoon.

1 small onion, minced
1/4 cup green pepper, cored, seeded, and chopped
1/4 cup celery, chopped

Add onion, green pepper and celery; brown lightly.

1 cup water
1/2 teaspoon salt
3/4 cup cooked rice
2 cups tomatoes, undrained
1 teaspoon sugar
1/4 teaspoon Worcestershire sauce
1 cup cheddar cheese, shredded

Stir in rice, tomatoes, sugar and Worcestershire sauce. Crumble bacon and stir into rice mixture; sprinkle cheese over top. Cover and continue cooking until cheese is melted, about 5 minutes.

CHINESE SAUSAGE RICE

Preparation and Cooking Time: 30 minutes   **Serves 2**

One of the simplest Chinese meals you can make. Chinese sausages are unique, and can be bought only in Chinese groceries. These sausages are well seasoned with soy sauce, Chinese spices and alcohol. There are two major types of Chinese sausages. Both are made with pork, but one is all pork, while the other is pork and duck livers.

INGREDIENTS	DIRECTIONS
2 cups uncooked rice, washed 1 pound (8 or 9 links) Chinese sausage	Wash rice and drain. Cover rice with enough water so that when your index finger is placed on top of the rice, the water will come just below the first joint of your index finger, about ¾ to 1 inch above the rice. Cover and bring rice to a vigorous boil; cook for 3 minutes. Bury sausage in the rice. Cover and reduce heat; cook for 20 minutes.
2 tablespoons soy sauce	Mix cooked rice with soy sauce. To serve, slice sausages diagonally into ⅛-inch slices. Serve hot.

SUSHI

Japanese Vinegared Rice

Preparation and Cooking Time: 1 hour   **Serves 6–8**

Sushi rice is the basis for a multitude of Japanese dishes.

INGREDIENTS
2 cups uncooked rice,
   washed and drained
2½ cups water

DIRECTIONS
Combine rice and water in an enameled saucepan and let rice soak for 30 minutes.

1 3-inch piece of kombu
   (seaweed), washed under
   cold running water
   (optional)

Add kombu to rice if available and bring to a rolling boil. Lower heat and cook until rice is tender and water is absorbed, about 20 minutes. Remove from heat and let rice rest for 4–5 minutes. Discard kombu. Pour rice into large shallow pan.

To make vinegar dressing:
¼ cup rice wine vinegar
   or 3 tablespoons mild
   white vinegar
¼ cup sugar
1 teaspoon salt

Mix vinegar with sugar and salt. Pour over rice; mix lightly with a fork and cool. Rice is ready to be used when it has reached room temperature.

WEST INDIES RICE

Preparation and Cooking Time: 1 hour 30 minutes **Serves 6**

Shredded coconut is the important ingredient.

INGREDIENTS	DIRECTIONS
2 cups shredded coconut 3 cups milk 2 tablespoons oil 1 medium onion, chopped	Soak coconut in milk for 1 hour. Simmer for 10 minutes; drain coconut, reserving milk. Squeeze out all milk. Sauté onion until limp and golden.
2 cups uncooked rice Salt to taste	Add reserved coconut milk, rice and salt; simmer for 20 minutes or until liquid is absorbed.
Cinnamon	Sprinkle with cinnamon and serve.

ARROZ VALENCIANA

Preparation and Cooking Time: 30 minutes   Serves 4–6

Mrs. Shelly (Irma) Balsam brought this classic Spanish rice dish with her from South America. Achote adds color, not flavor.

INGREDIENTS	DIRECTIONS
½ pound chorizo (Spanish sausage), cut in ¾-inch pieces	Fry sausage until well-cooked and browned. Remove sausage and keep warm.
1 teaspoon achote	If necessary, add enough oil to the pan to make 2 tablespoons oil. Add achote and cook until oil is red.
4 cups hot cooked rice 1 cup hot cooked peas 2 tablespoons slivered carrot Salt and freshly ground black pepper to taste 4 hard-boiled eggs, quartered	Mix oil and cooked chorizo with rice, peas and carrot. Season to taste. Arrange quartered eggs on top. Serve immediately.

ROZ'S WILD RICE CASSEROLE

Preparation and Baking Time: 1 hour 15 minutes ...**Serves 4**

A can of mushroom soup, sautéed vegetables and a wild rice mix make this easy and delicious casserole.

INGREDIENTS
- 4 tablespoons butter
- 1 large onion, chopped
- 1 cup diced celery
- 2 cups fresh mushrooms, sliced, or 2 3-ounce cans mushrooms, drained
- 1 teaspoon salt
- 1/4 teaspoon freshly ground black pepper

- 1/2 10 1/2-ounce can mushroom soup

- 2 1/2 cups cooked long-grain and wild-rice mix

DIRECTIONS
Sauté onions, celery, mushrooms, salt and black pepper in butter in a skillet until onions are limp and golden.

Add soup to vegetable mixture; mix well.

In a buttered casserole, alternate layers of rice and vegetable mixture. Cover and bake for 1 hour at 350° F.

CURRIED FRUIT ON RICE

Preparation and Cooking Time: 15 minutes   Serves 4–6

An ideal dish for a summer luncheon. A hot curry sauce is poured over sliced fruit and hot rice.

INGREDIENTS
1 cup chicken broth
1 cup white wine
1 cup raisins
1 cup pignolia nuts

DIRECTIONS
Combine chicken broth and wine in a saucepan. Heat to a boil and add raisiss and nuts. Reduce heat. Simmer for 5 minutes.

¼ cup chicken broth
¼ cup white wine
1½ tablespoons curry powder
1 tablespoon cornstarch
Pinch of salt

Mix curry powder with cornstarch, salt and remaining broth and wine. Stir into simmering sauce. Cook, stirring constantly, until sauce thickens and clears. Taste and adjust seasoning if necessary.

4 cups hot cooked rice

To serve, spoon hot rice into soup plates.

Suggested fruit
2 bananas, sliced
2 canned or fresh peaches, sliced
4 slices pineapple
½ cup grated coconut

Arrange chosen fruit on top of rice. Pour hot curry sauce over top. Sprinkle with coconut and serve.

52

RICE CEREAL

Preparation and Cooking Time: 30 minutes   **Serves 4**

Brown rice would be especially good in this dish because of its nutty taste.

INGREDIENTS
1 cup uncooked rice
2 cups water
1/2 teaspoon salt

DIRECTIONS
Cook rice in salted boiling water over a medium heat until rice is tender and all liquid has been absorbed.

2 tablespoons honey
1/2 cup pineapple juice
1/2 cup pineapple cubes
1/2 cup diced apricots or peaches
1/2 cup fresh seasonal berries or frozen sliced strawberries

Add honey, pineapple juice, pineapple cubes, apricots and berries. Cook for about 7–8 minutes, until fruits are hot.

Light cream

Serve topped with light cream.

Rice
with
Eggs
and
Cheese

❧

INDIAN FRIED RICE BALLS

Preparation and Cooking Time: 20 minutes   Serves 4

These delicious tidbits from India can be frozen and reheated for serving.

INGREDIENTS
2 cups cooked rice
1 cup grated cheddar
  cheese
Mustard

Oil for frying

DIRECTIONS
Mix rice and cheese together; form into balls the size of large walnuts. Spread outside with prepared mustard.

Fry in oil.

RICE CROQUETTES

Preparation and Cooking Time: 30 minutes   Serves 4

Rice croquettes go with everything—chicken, meat or fish.

INGREDIENTS
4 cups cooked rice
3 tablespoons freshly
  grated Romano cheese

DIRECTIONS
In a large bowl mix together rice, cheese, parsley and black pep-

1 teaspoon minced fresh
parsley
1/8 teaspoon freshly
ground black pepper
2 or 3 medium eggs

per; add 1 egg at a time
until mixture sticks to-
gether. Wet hands in oil
or egg white; shape rice
into oblong or round cro-
quettes.

Dry seasoned bread crumbs

Roll croquettes in bread
crumbs.

Oil for frying

Heat ¼-inch oil in a skillet; fry croquettes until
golden brown all over.
Drain on absorbent pa-
per.

VARIATIONS
Add cubed prosciutto,
salami or mozzarella in
the center of each cro-
quette for an extra sur-
prise.

BAKED RICE AND CHEDDAR CHEESE

Preparation and Cooking Time: 25 minutes   **Serves 4**

If you like macaroni and cheese, you should like this.

INGREDIENTS
3 cups cooked rice
3 tablespoons butter
1/4 pound mild cheddar
cheese, grated
2 cups milk
1 tablespoon minced fresh
parsley

DIRECTIONS
Mix together rice, butter,
cheddar cheese, milk,
parsley, onion and ham.
Season with salt and pep-
per. Pour into a baking
dish.

1 tablespoon grated onion
1/2 cup chopped ham
Salt and freshly ground
   black pepper to taste

Cracker crumbs

Cover top with crumbs
and bake at 350° F. until
brown and bubbly, about
20 minutes. Add more
milk if dish becomes too
dry.

BAKED RICE WITH CHEESE

Preparation and Baking Time: 20 minutes   Serves 4

Curry-flavored, toasted bread cubes are a delicious and
unusual addition to this dish.

INGREDIENTS
3 cups cooked rice
3/4 cup grated cheddar
   cheese

DIRECTIONS
Spoon half the rice into a
greased baking dish.
Sprinkle with part of the
cheese. Repeat. Bake at
350° F. until rice is hot
and cheese melts, about
15 minutes.

To make bread cubes:
3 tablespoons butter or
   margarine
1/2 teaspoon curry powder
1 slice white bread, cut
   into small cubes

Meanwhile, melt butter
in a small skillet; stir in
curry. Add bread cubes
and brown lightly. Sprin-
kle over hot rice dish before serving.

RICE WITH CHEESE

Preparation and Cooking Time: 10 minutes*   **Serves 4**

Delicious with lamb or pork.

INGREDIENTS
- 3 tablespoons butter
- 4 cups cooked rice
- 2 tablespoons freshly grated Romano cheese
- 1/8 teaspoon freshly ground black pepper

DIRECTIONS
Heat butter in a large skillet; add rice, cheese and black pepper, and stir gently with a fork until well heated. You can also put ingredients in a pie plate and bake 20 minutes at 400° F.

*When prepared in skillet.

RICE WITH LEMON AND EGG

Preparation and Cooking Time: 25 minutes   **Serves 4**

Complements fish or an omelet.

INGREDIENTS
- 1 cup uncooked rice, cooked al dente and drained
- 2 tablespoons butter
- 3 eggs, beaten
- 1/2 cup freshly grated Parmesan cheese
- Juice of 1 lemon

DIRECTIONS
When rice is cooked, melt butter in a large skillet; add drained rice. Beat eggs, cheese and lemon juice together; pour this mixture into the rice and cook, stirring constantly, over low heat

for 3–4 minutes. Serve at once while rice is still creamy.

BAKED RICE PIE

Preparation and Cooking Time: 30 minutes   Serves 4

This is a marvelous recipe to use up leftovers.

INGREDIENTS
4 cups cooked rice
½ cup freshly grated Romano cheese
¼ teaspoon freshly ground black pepper
3 eggs, beaten
2 tablespoons butter
½ pound mozzarella, cubed

DIRECTIONS
Mix together in a large bowl rice, grated cheese, black pepper and eggs. Put in a buttered 9-inch pie plate; top with dots of butter and cubed mozzarella. Bake for 20 minutes at 400°F. Slice and serve like pie.

VARIATIONS
Add chopped, cooked sausage, salami, prosciutto or ham.

Instead of rice, use mashed potatoes or cooked spaghetti which has been broken into 1-inch lengths before cooking.

RICE OMELET

Preparation and Cooking Time: 30 minutes **Serves 4**

Rice is an almost nutlike addition to an omelet. Here it is flavored with freshly grated Parmesan cheese.

INGREDIENTS
1/2 cup rice
2 cups milk

DIRECTIONS
Cook rice in milk until tender, about 14 minutes. Cool.

2 tablespoons butter
2 tablespoons freshly grated Parmesan cheese
4 egg yolks
Salt and freshly ground black pepper to taste

Mix together rice with butter, grated cheese, egg yolks; salt and pepper to taste.

4 egg whites, beaten stiff
1/4 cup freshly grated Parmesan cheese
2 tablespoons butter

Fold into egg whites the rice mixture and grated cheese; cook gently in buttered omelet pan. When almost cooked, fold in half and serve immediately.

CHEESE AND RICE SOUFFLE

Preparation and Cooking Time: 1 hour   **Serves 4–6**

Serve at once when done.

INGREDIENTS

2 tablespoons butter or margarine
3 tablespoons flour
¾ cup milk

DIRECTIONS

Combine butter and flour in a saucepan; stir over low heat until smooth. Gradually add milk; cook, stirring constantly, until thickened.

4 egg yolks, beaten
1 cup cooked rice

Add beaten egg yolks slowly to mixture, stirring constantly. Remove from heat and stir in rice. Cool slightly.

4 egg whites, beaten until stiff

Beat egg whites until stiff. Gently fold into cheese-rice mixture. Turn into a greased 1½-quart soufflé dish or straight-sided casserole. Bake, uncovered, in a 325° F. oven for 35–40 minutes until golden brown. Serve at once.

POACHED EGGS BENEDICT ON RICE

Preparation and Cooking Time: **Serves 3**

Serve this classic dish on seasoned rice instead of the traditional English muffin.

INGREDIENTS
To make rice:
3 cups hot cooked rice
1/4 cup freshly grated
     Romano cheese
2 tablespoons butter
     freshly ground black
     pepper to taste

DIRECTIONS
Season rice with grated cheese, butter and black pepper.

6 slices ham
2 tablespoons butter
6 eggs

Sauté ham in butter. Poach the eggs. Place each slice of ham on a rice nest and top with a poached egg.

To make Hollandaise Sauce:
1/4 cup butter, at room
     temperature
4 egg yolks, beaten
2 tablespoons lemon juice
Salt and freshly ground
     black pepper

Melt ¼ cup butter in the top of a double boiler over hot, not boiling water. Add egg yolks and lemon juice. Beat constantly with a wire whisk until butter is melted. Add another ¼ cup butter and stir. When sauce thickens, add another ¼ cup butter. Continue stirring until butter is absorbed. Add the last ¼ cup butter; stir and cook until sauce has thickened. Season to taste.

Note: Should the sauce curdle; add 2 tablespoons boiling water, beating constantly to remake the emulsion.

Seafood
with
Rice

❧

JAPANESE RAW FISH RICE BALLS

Preparation Time: 20 minutes*

Serves 4

Substitute smoked salmon for the raw fish.

INGREDIENTS
3 ounces tuna, mackerel, whitefish, fluke or other white-meat fish fillet, cut crosswise into paper-thin slices
Salt

½ cup sushi rice (see page   )
Toasted sesame seeds
Soy sauce

DIRECTIONS
Slice fish crosswise into paper-thin slices. Cut slices 2 inches long by 1 inch wide. Sprinkle with salt. Let marinate at room temperature for 3 hours.

To make fish balls, take 1 tablespoon of Sushi rice and form it into an oval. Place a slice of fish on top and mold it as symmetrically as possible. Sprinkle with sesame seeds. Serve with soy sauce.

*Does not include Marinating Time.

VARIATION
Substitute smoked salmon
for raw fish.

CRAB CROQUETTES

Preparation and Cooking Time: 45 minutes   **Serves 4**

Serve with a mushroom sauce.

INGREDIENTS
4 tablespoons butter
1/4 cup flour
1 cup milk
1 teaspoon mustard
Pinch of oregano

DIRECTIONS
Melt butter in a saucepan; stir flour into butter. When smooth, add milk, stirring constantly. Add mustard and oregano. Cook, stirring constantly, until thickened.

1 cup crab meat, drained
  and flaked
1 canned pimiento,
  chopped
3 cups cooked rice
Salt and freshly ground
  black pepper to taste
Butter

Stir in crab meat, pimiento and rice. Season with salt and pepper to taste. Shape into 4 croquettes. Place on buttered baking pan. Dot with butter. Bake for 30 minutes at 375° F., turning once to brown other side. Serve with mushroom sauce.

To make mushroom sauce:
2 tablespoons butter
1 small onion, minced

Cook mushrooms and onion in butter in a skillet

½ pound fresh mushrooms, sliced	until onion is limp and golden. Push vegetables to one side of skillet.
2 tablespoons flour	Stir in flour.
½ cup cream ½ cup sour cream 2 tablespoons sherry Salt and freshly ground black pepper to taste	When smooth, add cream, sour cream, sherry, salt and pepper. Stir and mix thoroughly. Serve hot over croquettes.

SUGGESTED MENU
Crab Croquettes
Chilled Broccoli
    with Oil and Lemon

Italian Lemon Ice
Cookies

TUNA CROQUETTES

Preparation and Cooking Time: 20 minutes   Serves 4–6

Economical and good.

INGREDIENTS
1 6-ounce can tuna, drained
2 cups cooked rice
1 tablespoon minced fresh parsley
1 egg
2 tablespoons milk

DIRECTIONS
Combine tuna, rice, parsley, egg, milk, salt and mustard. Mix thoroughly.

71

1/4 teaspoon salt
1/8 teaspoon prepared
   mustard

Cracker meal

Shape into cakes and roll in cracker meal.

Oil for frying

Fry cakes on each side until golden brown. Drain on absorbent paper.

SUGGESTED MENU
Tuna Croquettes
Molded Grapefruit Salad

Fresh Fruit
Coffee

CODFISH CAKES

Preparation and Cooking Time: 20 minutes   **Serves 4**

Cod was once one of the main sources of food for New England. Here's a variation on ever-popular codfish cakes.

INGREDIENTS
2 cups cooked flaked codfish or other firm-bodied white fish
2 cups cooked rice
2 teaspoons minced onion
1/4 cup minced fresh parsley
3 tablespoons butter, at room temperature

DIRECTIONS
Combine fish, potatoes, onion, parsley and butter together in a large bowl. Add milk and mix together. Then add eggs one at a time. Mixture should not be too loose or cakes will fall apart when

1/2 cup milk 3 medium eggs	fried. Shape into small, round, flat cakes or balls.
Dry seasoned bread crumbs	Roll in bread crumbs and chill thoroughly before frying.
Oil for frying	Heat at least ¼ inch of oil in a heavy frying pan. When hot, add cakes; cook, turning once, over a medium heat until nicely browned. Drain on absorbent paper before serving.

SUGGESTED MENU
Clam Chowder

Codfish and Rice Cakes
Celery
Bread-and-Butter Pickles
Blueberry Muffins

Bread Pudding

FISH AND LOBSTER CASSEROLE

Preparation and Cooking Time: 45 minutes   **Serves 4**

Use all fish if your budget prohibits buying lobster.

INGREDIENTS	DIRECTIONS
3 tablespoons butter 1 tablespoon minced onion 1 tablespoon minced green pepper	Sauté onion and green pepper in butter until onion is limp and golden; push to one side.

73

2 tablespoons flour 1 cup milk ½ cup cream	Blend in flour; add milk and cream and cook, stirring constantly, until thickened.
1½ cups cooked rice 1 cup flaked cooked fish ½ cup cooked lobster meat, 1 tablespoon minced pimiento, 1 tablespoon sherry 3 tablespoons shredded mild Cheddar cheese ½ teaspoon salt ⅛ teaspoon freshly ground black pepper	Mix rice, fish, lobster meat, pimiento, cheese, sherry, salt and pepper with sauce. Put into a buttered baking dish.
½ cup buttered bread crumbs	Sprinkle with bread crumbs. Bake for 30 minutes at 350° F.

SUGGESTED MENU
*Fish and Lobster
    Casserole*
Sliced Tomato Salad

Lime Pie
Coffee

FISH AND RICE RAMEKINS

Preparation and Cooking Time: 30 minutes   **Serves 4**

Perfect for a ladies' luncheon.

INGREDIENTS
1 cup cooked rice
2 tablespoons butter, melted
1/4 cup freshly grated Parmesan cheese
1 cup cooked fish, shrimps, scallops or crab meat

DIRECTIONS
Mixed cooked rice with melted butter and cheese; fold in cooked fish. Butter four ramekins; put in layer of rice mixture. Set aside.

To make sauce:
1 tablespoon flour
1 tablespoon butter
Salt and freshly ground black pepper
1/2 cup warm milk

Stir flour into melted butter to make a roux; slowly add warm milk, stirring constantly, until thick and smooth. Season with salt and pepper to taste.

1 egg, beaten

As sauce thickens, remove from heat and add beaten egg first to a little sauce and then to entire mixture.

1/4 cup freshly grated Parmesan cheese
1 talespoon butter

Pour cream sauce over ramekins; sprinkle with grated cheese and dot with butter. Bake at 400° F. for 10 minutes or un-

til bubbly and lightly
browned.

SUGGESTED MENU
Fish and Rice Ramekins
Chilled Asparagus
    with Oil and Lemon

Fresh Pineapple
Tea

FISH CASSEROLE

Preparation and Baking Time: 45 minutes   **Serves 4**

Leftover fish mixed with rice and sherry makes an exceptionally delicious luncheon dish.

INGREDIENTS
3 tablespoons butter or
    margarine
1 tablespoon chopped
    onion
1 tablespoon chopped
    green pepper

2 tablespoons flour
1 cup milk
½ cup cream

1½ cups cooked rice
1½ cups flaked cooked fish
1 tablespoon minced

DIRECTIONS
Sauté onion and green
pepper in melted butter
until limp; push to one
side of the skillet.

Blend flour into butter to
make a roux; add milk
and cream, stirring constantly, until smooth and
thick.

Mix with sauce rice, fish
pimiento, cheese, sherry,
salt and black pepper;

pimiento
3 tablespoons shredded
  cheddar cheese
1 tablespoon sherry
1/2 teaspoon salt
1/4 teaspoon freshly ground
  black pepper

1/2 cup buttered bread
  crumbs

spoon into a buttered
baking dish.

Cover with buttered
bread crumbs; bake for
30 minutes in a 350° F.
oven or until brown and
bubbly.

SUGGESTED MENU
Fish Casserole
Mixed Green Salad
Celery Seed Biscuits

Orange Jello
  with Whipped Cream
Coffee

RICE-STUFFED FLOUNDER ROLLS

Preparation and Baking Time: 40 minutes   Serves 4

Baked flounder takes on new importance when stuffed with
rice and clams in this recipe concocted by Mrs. George
(Barbara) Davidson.

INGREDIENTS
2 tablespoons butter
1 10½-ounce can minced
  clams, drained
1/2 cup cooked rice
1/4 cup cooked rice

DIRECTIONS
Melt butter in a large
saucepan. Add clams,
rice, bread crumbs,
parsley, onion flakes,
lemon juice and garlic

77

¼ cup seasoned bread crumbs
1 teaspoon dried parsley
1 teaspoon minced onion flakes
3 teaspoons reconstituted lemon juice
½ teaspoon garlic salt

salt. Toss lightly over low heat for 1 minute or until ingredients are well blended. Remove from heat.

1½ pounds flounder filets washed and drained

Spread 2 tablespoons of clam-rice filling on top of each flounder filet. Roll up jellyroll fashion, starting with the widest end of the filet.

2 tablespoons butter
¼ cup white wine

Place flounder rolls in a single layer in a greased baking pan. Dot each roll with butter; pour white wine over all. Bake uncovered in a preheated 350° F. oven for 25 minutes or until fish flakes easily.

Fresh parsley
Lemon wedges

Remove carefully to heated serving platter; pour liquid from pan over the top. Garnish with fresh parsley and lemon wedges; serve immediately.

SUGGESTED MENU
Rice-Stuffed Flounder Rolls
String Beans with Almonds

Lemon Pound Cake
Coffee

BAKED FISH WITH RICE TOMATO STUFFING

Preparation and Cooking Time: 1 hour   **Serves 4–6**

An excellent stuffing of rice and tomatoes makes this simple fish dish superb.

INGREDIENTS	DIRECTIONS
1 3-pound haddock or any firm-bodied baking fish, cleaned Salt	After cleaning fish (remove head if desired), rub both outside and inside with salt. Slit almost the whole length of fish. Fill with the following stuffing.

To make stuffing:

1½ cups cooked rice 2 cups canned tomatoes, undrained 1 small onion, minced ½ teaspoon salt ⅛ teaspoon freshly ground black pepper ½ teaspoon curry powder	Mix together rice, tomatoes, onion, salt, pepper and curry powder. Stuff fish and lay in a greased baking dish. Fasten fish together with small skewers.
Strips of salt pork	Gash fish crosswise on top and insert salt pork. Bake for 45 minutes or until fish flakes easily in a 400° F. oven.

79

SUGGESTED MENU
*Baked Fish
with Rice-Tomato Stuf-
fing*

Tossed Salad with Avo-
cado
Napoleons
Coffee

BAKED FISH WITH RICE

Preparation and Cooking Time: 40 minutes   **Serves 4**

Fish steaks are baked on a bed of rice flavored with onion and paprika.

INGREDIENTS	DIRECTIONS
4 tablespoons salt pork, diced 1 large onion, chopped	Sauté salt pork until almost done; add onion and cook until limp and golden.
1½ cups cooked rice	Stir in cooked rice; spread on the bottom of a baking dish.
2 pounds fish steaks	Arrange fish in a single layer on top of the rice mixture. Sprinkle with paprika. Bake in a moderately hot oven 375° F. oven for 15 minutes. Turn fish and bake for 15 minutes longer.

SUGGESTED MENU
Baked Fish with Rice
Broiled Tomatoes

Cherry Tart
Coffee

SALMON AND RICE RING

Preparation and Cooking Time: 1 hour 10 minutes

Serves 4-6

A light luncheon dish.

INGREDIENTS	DIRECTIONS
1 tablespoon fresh chopped parsley 1 teaspoon grated onion 1 tablespoon lemon juice ¼ cup milk.	Combine parsley, onion, lemon juice and milk.
2 eggs 2 cups canned salmon Salt and freshly ground black pepper to taste	Add beaten eggs and salmon. Season with salt and pepper.
3 cups cooked rice	Place layer of rice in a greased ring mold; cover with half of salmon mixture. Repeat. Place in a pan of hot water; bake in 325° F. oven for 1 hour.

SUGGESTED MENU
Salmon and Rice Ring
Buttered Asparagus
Peaches in Wine
Coffee

AFRICAN FISH STEW

Preparation and Cooking Time: 1 hour*   **Serves 4**

West Africans serve a variety of starches with their stews—corn, rice plantain, and yams. They are the mainstay of the diet; the amount of sauce, stew, or soup accompanying the starch depends on the individual family's economic situation.

INGREDIENTS
- 1 teaspoon salt
- 1 teaspoon cayenne pepper
- 1 red bell pepper, seeded and sliced
- 1/2 cup lemon juice
- 2 tablespoons vinegar
- 1 tablespoon peanut oil
- 1 1/2 pounds fish fillets
- 2 medium onions, sliced

- 2 tablespoons peanut oil
- 1 cup water

DIRECTIONS
Combine salt, cayenne pepper, pepper slices, lemon juice, vinegar and peanut oil.

Pour over fish and sliced onions in a bowl. Marinate 6 hours. Drain fish and onions, reserving marinade.

When ready to prepare dish, broil fish on an oiled pan until golden on both sides. Heat peanut oil in a deep skillet and sauté drained marinated onions until limp and golden. Add marinade, grilled fish and 1 cup water. Cover and cook over low heat 10 minutes.

*Does not include Marinating Time.

4 cups hot cooked rice   Serve over dry cooked rice.

SUGGESTED MENU
African Fish Stew
Fruit Compote
Coffee

JAPANESE RICE WITH SHRIMP AND VEGETABLES

Preparation and Cooking Time: 30 minutes   **Serves 4–6**

Try and cut the vegetables evenly.

INGREDIENTS	DIRECTIONS
1 pound fresh shrimp, shelled, deveined, and cut in half 2 tablespoons oil	Prepare shrimps. Heat oil in a large skillet. Add shrimp and sauté until they turn pink, turning once or twice.
1 large carrot, cut into thin strips 2 scallions with tops, sliced 1 cup coarsely chopped fresh spinach 3 tablespoons soy sauce 3 tablespoons fish or chicken broth 1 teaspoon sugar	Add carrots, scallions, spinach, stock, soy sauce and sugar. Cook mixture over low heat for 5 minutes.
4 cups hot cooked rice	Stir in hot rice and cook for 1 minute longer. Serve immediately.

83

SUGGESTED MENU
*Japanese Rice with
Shrimp and Vegetables*

Sliced Pineapple
Tea

SHRIMP AND EGGPLANT CREOLE

Preparation and Cooking Time: 1 hour   **Serves 4–6**

Absolutely the best!

INGREDIENTS
1/2 cup butter
2 cups chopped onion
1 cup chopped green
  pepper
1 cup chopped celery

2 garlic cloves, minced
1 2-pound 3-ounce can
  plum tomatoes,
  undrained
1 8-ounce can tomato
  paste
1 teaspoon salt
1/4 teaspoon freshly
  ground black pepper
1 teaspoon Worcestershire
  sauce
1 bay leaf
1/2 teaspoon thyme
3 slices lemon peel
2 whole cloves
Pinch of sugar

DIRECTIONS
Heat butter in a heavy
Dutch oven; add onion,
green pepper and celery.
Sauté until onion is limp
and golden.

Add garlic, tomatoes, to-
mato paste, salt, pepper,
Worcestershire sauce, bay
leaf, thyme, lemon peel,
cloves and sugar. Simmer
for 10 minutes.

1/4 cup olive oil 1 medium eggplant, diced, with skin left on	Heat olive oil in a skillet; sauté eggplant until almost done. Reserve.
1 1/2 pounds shrimp, shelled and deveined with tails left on	Add shrimp to tomato mixture and simmer for 10 minutes more. Then add sautéed eggplant and cook for 10 minutes more. Discard lemon peel and bay leaf.
2 tablespoons minced fresh parsley 1 tablespoon capers	Stir in parsley and capers. Serve over rice.

To make rice:

2 tablespoons butter 1 tablespoon minced onion 1 small garlic clove, minced	Sauté onion and garlic in butter until limp.
1 cup uncooked rice 2 1/4 cups boiling chicken stock Dash of tabasco sauce	Add rice, chicken stock and tabasco sauce. Cover and simmer for 20 minutes.

SUGGESTED MENU
Shrimp and Eggplant Creole
Corn Bread

Chocolate Chess Pie
Coffee

RICE WITH SHRIMP

Preparation and Cooking Time: 30 minutes   **Serves 4**

Rice simmered in a fish stock is a delicate rice dish.

INGREDIENTS
DIRECTIONS

2 tablespoons olive oil
2 tablespoons butter
1 garlic clove, minced
1 teaspoon minced fresh
  parsley
1 cup uncooked rice

Sauté garlic, parsley and rice in olive oil and butter in a large skillet until golden.

1 cup fish stock or clam
  broth

Add stock and cover; simmer until stock is almost evaporated, about 5 minutes.

2½ cups fish stock or clam
  broth
¾ pound fresh shrimp,
  shelled and deveined,
  or frozen shrimp,
  thawed and drained

Add rest of stock and shrimp; cover and simmer until liquid is almost gone and shrimp are pink, about 10 minutes. Add more stock if necessary as dish should be slightly moist.

1 tablespoon butter or oil
¼ cup freshly grated
  Parmesan cheese

Toss with grated cheese and butter; let stand for 3 minutes before serving.

SUGGESTED MENU
Rice with Shrimp
Stuffed Zucchini
Celery and Olives

Raspberry Tart
Coffee

SHRIMP AND WILD RICE CASSEROLE

Preparation and Baking Time: 30 minutes   **Serves 4**

An easy-to-prepare wild rice casserole of shrimp, mushrooms and cream of chicken soup.

INGREDIENTS
2½ cups cooked wild rice
    or wild rice mix
1 10½-ounce can cream
    of chicken soup
¾ cup dry white wine
1 3-ounce can sliced
    mushrooms, drained
2 cups chopped cooked
    shrimp or any leftover
    seafood

Fresh parsley

DIRECTIONS
Combine cooked rice,
soup, wine, mushrooms
and shrimp; pour into a
casserole. Bake at 325° F.
for 20 minutes or until
hot and bubbly.

Garnish with fresh
parsley and serve imme-
diately.

SUGGESTED MENU
Caesar's Salad
*Shrimp and Wild Rice
    Casserole*

Chocolate Cake à la mode
Coffee

SHRIMP NEWBURG

Preparation and Cooking Time: 15 minutes   **Serves 4**

Delicately flavored with sherry.

INGREDIENTS	DIRECTIONS
1/4 cup butter or margarine 2 1/2 tablespoons flour 3/4 teaspoon salt Dash of cayenne pepper Dash of nutmeg	Blend flour and seasonings in melted butter either in a saucepan or a chafing dish.
3 cups cream 3 tablespoons sherry	Stir in cream and sherry gradually; cook until thickened and smooth, stirring constantly.
2 egg yolks, beaten	Mix a little of the hot sauce into egg yolks; then add to sauce, stirring constantly.
2 cups chopped, cooked shrimps 4 cups hot cooked rice	Add shrimp and heat; serve immediately with rice.

SUGGESTED MENU
*Shrimp Newburg
    with Rice*
Popovers

Strawberries in Wine
Coffee

TENDON

Tempura over Rice

Preparation and Cooking Time: 1 hour 30 minutes   **Serves 4**

Tendon, in its simplest form, is shrimps or other seafood and vegetables fried like tempura, but served on a bed of rice. Sauce is poured over the top.

INGREDIENTS
1 pound large fresh
shrimps, shelled and
deveined

DIRECTIONS
Have shrimp cleaned in the fish store or do it yourself. Shell the shrimp, but leave the tail attached. Split each shrimp down the back and remove the black intestinal vein. Wash in cold water; dry on absorbent paper. Set aside.

Suggested vegetables:
4 large fresh mushrooms
Watercress, whole sprigs
1 medium carrot, cleaned
and cut into 1/4-inch
vertical strips
4 small scallions with green
top, cut into 2-inch-long
pieces
Spinach, whole perfect
leaves

All the ingredients must be prepared before you begin to fry. Clean vegetables. The choice of vegetables depends entirely upon what you have available. Great care should be taken to cut the vegetables evenly.

To make batter:
1 large egg
1 cup ice-cold water
1/4 teaspoon sugar
1/8 teaspoon baking soda
1 cup flour

Beat egg and ice-cold water together in a mixing bowl; add sugar and baking soda. Gradually mix in flour with a whisk or fork. Do not overmix. The batter should be lumpy.

Oil for frying

Fill a deep frying pan with 2 inches of oil. Heat oil until hot.

To test, dip one shrimp into batter and place in oil. If oil bubbles, it is hot enough to begin frying. Fry shrimp and vegetables until light golden brown. Remove from pan and drain on absorbent paper.

Be careful of spattering oil. If oil gets too hot or smoky, lower heat. Skim particles of fried batter with a mesh skimmer once in a while, as these will burn and discolor the oil.

To make sauce:
1 cup dashi (fish seafood stock)
1/3 cup soy sauce
1/3 cup sake
Sugar to taste

Combine stock, soy sauce, sake and sugar; mix well.

4 cups hot cooked rice

To serve, place fried seafood and vegetables on top of a bed of rice. Sauce is poured over all.

SUGGESTED MENU
Tendon

Tangerines
Cookies
Tea

SHRIMP WITH TOMATOES, ONIONS AND PEPPERS

Preparation and cooking Time: 45 minutes*   **Serves 4**

My brother-in-law, Michael Torre, developed this recipe for shrimp simmered in a thick tomato sauce filled with onions and peppers.

INGREDIENTS

1 pound fresh medium shrimps, shelled and deveined, or 1 pound cleaned frozen shrimp, thawed and drained

DIRECTIONS

Have shrimp cleaned in the fish store or do it yourself. Shell the shrimp and remove the tail; split each shrimp down the back and remove the black intestinal vein. Wash in cold water; dry on absorbent paper. Set aside.

**2 tablespoons olive oil
2 medium onions, coarsely chopped**

Heat olive oil in a medium-sized pot; sauté onions and peppers, stir-

*Does not include time to clean shrimp.

91

2 medium green peppers, cored, seeded and coarsely chopped

3 fresh tomatoes, cored, seeded and coarsely chopped or ½ cup tomato sauce

½ teaspoon salt

⅛ teaspoon freshly ground black pepper

ring occasionally, until onions are limp and the peppers slightly brown, about 10 minutes. Add tomatoes or sauce to pot; cook, stirring occasionally, for about 15 minutes or until it becomes dry and almost sticks to the pan. Add cleaned shrimp, salt and black pepper; cook, stirring occasionally, for at least 10 minutes or until the shrimps turn pink.

4 cups hot cooked rice

This is delicious served over rice or as a sandwich on Italian bread or with Italian hard biscuits.

SUGGESTED MENU
Shrimp with Tomatoes, Onions and Peppers over Rice
Romaine and Cucumber Salad

Sesame Seed Cookies
Espresso

RICE WITH CLAMS IN TOMATO

Preparation and Cooking Time: 45 minutes   **Serves 4**

Clams, which are cooked in their shells in tomato sauce,
are served over rice.

INGREDIENTS
- 2 tablespoons olive oil
- 1 garlic clove, chopped
- 1 8-ounce can tomato sauce
- 1 teaspoon minced fresh parsley
- 1/8 teaspoon freshly ground black pepper
- 1/8 teaspoon crushed red pepper

DIRECTIONS
Heat olive oil in a deep skillet; sauté garlic until limp. Add tomato sauce, parsley, black pepper and red pepper; simmer for 20 minutes until the sauce is thick and dry.

- 2 dozen small clams, scrubbed and washed thoroughly

While sauce is cooking, scrub clams with a stiff brush to remove sand; rinse in cold water three or four times. Add clams to sauce and cook for 10–15 minutes until they open.

- 2 cups uncooked rice, cooked al dente and drained

Serve sauce with clams over hot rice.

SUGGESTED MENU
Rice with Clams in Tomato

Lettuce, Cucumber and
Tomato Salad

Lemon Ice Assorted
Cookies
Espresso

CLAM RISOTTO

Preparation and Cooking Time: 20 minutes   **Serves 4**

If you use canned minced clams, this dish is a cinch to make.

INGREDIENTS	DIRECTIONS
5 tablespoons olive oil 2 garlic cloves, minced 2 tablespoons minced fresh parsley	Sauté garlic in oil with parsley until limp and golden.
1 10½-ounce can minced clams with juice, or 2 dozen clams, scrubbed 1 cup white wine 1 cup uncooked rice 1/8 teaspoon freshly ground black pepper	Add clams, rice, wine and black pepper; cover and simmer until almost absorbed, about 5 minutes.
2½ cups hot clam broth	Add broth; cover and cook until rice is done, about 10 minutes more. Dish should be moist. Serve immediately.

SUGGESTED MENU
Fried Filet of Flounder
Clam Risotto
Mixed Green Salad

Orange Sherbet and
Cookies
Coffee

MUSSELS WITH RICE

Preparation and Cooking Time: 45 minutes　　**Serves 4**

A touch of tomato and scallions add considerable flavor.

INGREDIENTS

2 dozen mussels

DIRECTIONS

Prepare mussels by covering with cold water and soaking for half an hour. Scrub with a stiff brush to remove all dirt and pull out hairy tuft if any shows. Rinse well. Reserve.

1 large bunch of scallions with tops, chopped
1/2 cup olive oil
1 teaspoon tomato paste
1/4 cup water

Sauté scallions in oil. Add tomato paste, water and mussels; cover and steam until mussels open. Discard any that do not open. Do not shell mussels.

2 1/2 cups boiling chicken stock or water
Salt to taste
1 cup uncooked rice

Add boiling stock, salt and rice. Cover and cook until rice is tender about 20 minutes.

SUGGESTED MENU
Mussels with Rice

Peppers, celery and Olive
Salad

Cheese Cake
Coffee

SCALLOPS WITH RICE

Preparation and Cooking Time: 50 minutes   **Serves 4**

There's no watching when you bake it.

INGREDIENTS	DIRECTIONS
1 medium onion, finely chopped 3 tablespoons butter	Sauté onion in butter until limp and golden.
1 pound scallops, washed	Wash scallops and add. Simmer for 15 minutes, turning occasionally. Reserve.
½ cup rice 2 tablespoons olive oil About 1 cut water Salt to taste	Brown rice in olive oil until golden; place in a casserole. Drain juice from scallops; add enough water to scallop juice to make 1½ cups juice. Season with salt. Pour over rice. Bake covered in a 400° F. oven for 20 minutes. Stir in scallops and onion and bake 10 minutes longer.

SEAFOOD WITH RICE

Chopped fresh parsley

Sprinkle with chopped parsley before serving.

SUGGESTED MENU
Scallops with Rice
Green Bean Salad

Strawberry Shortcake
Coffee

BRANDIED LOBSTER CASSEROLE

Preparation and Cooking Time: 45 minutes   Serves 4–6

Elegant and easy.

INGREDIENTS

1/2 cup butter or margarine
1/2 pound large mushrooms, sliced thin

1/4 cup grated onion
4 tomatoes, peeled and cut in wedges

2 cups diced cooked lobster meat
1/2 teaspoon salt
Dash of freshly ground black pepper
1/4 teaspoon bitters

2 cups heavy cream
2 tablespoons minced fresh parsley
1/4 cup brandy
4 cups cooked rice

DIRECTIONS

Melt butter and add mushrooms; sauté briefly until limp.

Add onion and tomatoes; sauté until sauce forms, about 5 minutes.

Add lobster, salt, pepper and bitters. Stir and cook for 1 minute.

Stir in the cream. When it bubbles, add parsley and brandy. Remove from heat. Line a 2-quart casserole with rice; pour

97

in the lobster mixture.
Bake at 350° F. for 20
minutes or until bubbly.

SUGGESTED MENU
*Brandied Lobster
    Casserole*
Asparagus with Oil and
    Lemon

Sliced Bananas and
    Oranges
Coffee

LOBSTER NEWBURG

Preparation and Cooking Time: 20 minutes   **Serves 4**

Absolutely elegant! Company fare in a hurry.

INGREDIENTS	DIRECTIONS
4 tablespoons butter 3 tablespoons flour 1/2 teaspoon salt 1/8 teaspoon nutmeg Dash of cayenne pepper 2 cups cooked lobster meat	Melt butter in a heavy skillet over very low heat. Combine flour, salt, nutmeg and cayenne pepper; sprinkle over lobster meat. Sauté lobster in butter briefly.
1 cup heavy cream 3 tablespoons sherry	Add cream stirring constantly. Add sherry slowly while stirring.
4 cups hot cooked rice	Serve at once with rice.

SUGGESTED MENU
Lobster Newburg
with Rice
Buttered Peas

Peach Melba
Coffee

CRAB MEAT AND LOBSTER IN RICE RING

Preparation and Cooking Time: I hour   **Serves 6**

A Southern favorite.

INGREDIENTS
2 tablespoons butter
2 small onions, minced
2 stalks of celery with leaves, diced
2 medium green peppers, diced
I medium carrot, diced
3 whole garlic cloves

2 tablespoons flour

1½ cups canned tomatoes
I teaspoon salt
⅛ teaspoon freshly ground black pepper
Dash of cayenne

I cup crab meat, flaked
1½ cups lobster meat, diced

DIRECTIONS
Melt butter in a heavy saucepan or Dutch oven. Add onion, celery, green pepper, carrot and garlic. Sauté over low heat until onions are limp and golden, about 15 minutes. Remove whole garlic cloves and discard.

Blend in flour.

Add tomatoes, salt, pepper and cayenne. Cook over medium heat for 20 minutes. Press through a sieve.

Add crab meat and lobster meat.
Simmer gently for 15

99

minutes. To serve spoon in center of rice ring.

To make rice ring:
6 cups hot cooked rice
2 tablespoons butter, at room temperature

Mix rice and butter with a fork and pack lightly into a well-buttered or oiled 1½-quart mold. Let stand 1 minute; then invert on a hot platter. Fill center with crab meat and lobster mixture.

Note: If dinner must be held, don't mold rice until the very last minute. It will keep hot in the pan far better than in the mold.

SUGGESTED MENU
Crab Meat and Lobster in Rice Ring
Popovers

Lemon Sherbet
Cookies
Coffee

Meats
with
Rice

❧

ARANCINI

Sicilian Rice Croquettes

Preparation and Cooking Time: 1 hour 45 minutes **Serves 6**

Sicily is famous for these rice croquettes filled with a meat sauce and peas.

INGREDIENTS

To make rice:
2 cups uncooked rice
1 quart chicken stock
1 teaspoon saffron

3 tablespoons butter, at room temperature

DIRECTIONS

Combine rice, chicken stock and saffron in a large kettle. When stock begins to boil, turn heat down low; stir rice once; cover kettle and simmer until all the liquid is absorbed, about 15 minutes. Rice should be slightly sticky so that it will hold together. Set rice aside to cool.

Add butter, eggs and grated cheese to cooled

2 eggs, beaten
1 cup freshly grated
Parmesan cheese

rice; stir well. Refrigerate.

To make filling:
1/4 cup olive oil
1 small onion, chopped
1/2 small stalk of celery, chopped
1/2 pound veal, beef or pork

Heat oil in saucepan and sauté onion and celery until onion is limp and golden.
Add meat and brown.

1 6-ounce can tomato paste
1 can water
1/2 teaspoon salt
1/4 teaspoon freshly ground black pepper

Stir in tomato paste, water, salt and pepper. Cover and simmer until meat is tender, for about 1 hour. Remove meat from sauce. Shred and return to sauce.

1/3 cup canned or frozen peas

Add peas and cook for 5 minutes longer. Cool.

To make croquettes:

Shape rice mixture into round balls (about ½ cup each). Make a hole in the rice balls with a stick or your finger; add 1 tablespoon filling and cover hole with more rice.

2 eggs, beaten
2 cups bread crumbs
Oil for frying

Dip croquettes into eggs and roll in bread crumbs until thoroughly coated. Fry a few at a time in 370° F. oil. Drain on absorbent paper. Serve warm or at room temperature.

BEEF STROGANOFF

Preparation and Cooking Time: 30 minutes   **Serves 4–6**

The beef must be brown on the outside yet beautifully rare within.

INGREDIENTS
2 pounds filet of beef, cut
  into 1-inch by 2-inch
  slices
4 tablespoons butter

DIRECTIONS
Heat butter in a heavy pan until sizzling. Add beef a few slices at a time, being careful that the pieces do not touch. Remove browned pieces and set aside until all beef is cooked.

¼ cup brandy

When meat is brown, put back into pan and pour brandy over the top and flame it. Remove meat from pan.

2 tablespoons butter
2 small garlic cloves,
  minced
1 cup sliced fresh
  mushrooms

Add butter, garlic and mushrooms to pan; sauté but do not allow garlic to brown. Remove from fire.

1 teaspoon tomato paste
3 tablespoons flour
½ cup beef stock

Stir in tomato paste, flour and stock. Stir over fire until it thickens, but don't let it boil.

1½ cups sour cream
2 tablespoons minced
  fresh dill

Add sour cream a little at a time, stirring constantly. Mix in dill and

105

heat the sauce until steaming but not boiling.

4 cups hot cooked rice
Add meat and serve with hot cooked rice.

SUGGESTED MENU
*Beef Stroganoff
with Rice*

Strawberry Parfait
Coffee

RICE AND BEEF PATTIES

Preparation and Cooking Time: 15 minutes   **Serves 4**

Ground beef and rice patties are browned first and then simmered in a sour cream gravy.

INGREDIENTS
1 pound ground beef
1 cup cooked rice
1 egg
2 strips bacon, cooked and crumbled
Add salt and freshly ground black pepper to taste

DIRECTIONS
Combine meat, rice, egg and crumbled bacon and season to taste. Shape into patties, brown on both sides until done. Remove from the pan to warm serving dish.

1 cup sour cream
2 tablespoons lemon juice

Add sour cream and lemon juice to pan; stir well, simmer for 1 minute and pour over patties. Serve hot.

SUGGESTED MENU
Rice and Beef Patties
Buttered String Beans

Strawberry Pie
Coffee

PICADILLO

Preparation and Cooking Time: 45 minutes   Serves 4-6

A Spanish mishmash of meat and raisins which is usually
served with rice and beans.

INGREDIENTS

DIRECTIONS

1 medium onion, minced
1 garlic clove, minced
4 tablespoons olive oil

Sauté onion and garlic in
the olive oil in a large
skillet until onion is
golden and limp.

1 pound ground beef
2 cups canned tomatoes,
   undrained
2 tablespoons raisins
1 teaspoon dry hot chili
   pepper or to taste
1 teaspoon vinegar
Salt and freshly ground
   black pepper to taste

Add beef, tomatoes, rais-
ins, chili pepper, vinegar,
salt and pepper. Simmer
for about 30 minutes.
Stew will be rather dry.

4 cups hot cooked rice
3 cups hot cooked black
   beans, red kidney beans,
   chick peas or pink
   Mexican beans
1 hard-boiled egg,
   chopped
Slivered almonds

Serve with rice and
beans.

Sprinkle the top with
chopped hard-boiled egg
and almonds.

107

SUGGESTED MENU
Picadillo
Rolls

Mango Cookies
Coffee

CHILI CON CARNE WITH RICE

Preparation and Cooking Time: 1 hour 30 minutes

Serves 4–6

Rice stretches this timeless favorite even further.

INGREDIENTS

2 tablespoons olive oil
1 pound ground beef
1 small onion, chopped
1 garlic clove, chopped
1 2-pound 3-ounce can Italian plum tomatoes
1 teaspoon salt
1 tablespoon minced fresh parsley
1/2 teaspoon basil
1/8 teaspoon freshly ground black pepper

1 16-ounce can red kidney beans, undrained
Pinch of crushed red pepper

DIRECTIONS

Heat olive oil in a medium-sized pot; sauté ground beef, onion and garlic, stirring frequently, until lightly browned. Pour off excess fat before straining tomatoes into pot. Season with salt, parsley, basil and black pepper. Simmer for 1 hour.

Add kidney beans and crushed red pepper 10 minutes before sauce is finished.

2 cups uncooked rice, cooked al dente and drained

½ cup freshly grated Parmesan cheese

Ladle just enough sauce over hot rice to cover each grain lightly. Sprinkle with cheese and toss at the table. Pass additional sauce and cheese.

SUGGESTED MENU
Chili Con Carne with Rice
Escarole Salad
Italian Bread

Sliced Peaches in Wine
Espresso

RICE LASAGNE

Preparation and Baking Time: 2 hours 30 minutes   **Serves 6**

Everybody's favorite is made with rice instead of pasta. This dish of rice baked with sausage sauce, mozzarella and grated cheese can be made early in the day and popped into the oven shortly before guests arrive.

INGREDIENTS
To make sauce:
1 pound Italian hot and/or sweet sausage, cut up

1 garlic clove, halved
1 2-pound 3-ounce can Italian plum tomatoes, undrained
1 teaspoon salt
½ teaspoon basil

DIRECTIONS
Fry sausage until brown and well cooked in a large saucepan.

Remove sausage and drain. Pour off all but 3 tablespoons of fat from pot; sauté garlic until limp. Add salt, basil, fennel seeds, black pepper

109

1/4 teaspoon fennel seeds
Pinch of freshly ground
   black pepper

and reserved sausage. Simmer for 1½ hours.

9 cups hot cooked rice

When sauce is almost done, cook rice *al dente* and drain. Set aside to cool slightly.

1 pound ricotta cheese
3 tablespoons freshly
   grated Parmesan cheese
2 eggs, beaten

Mix together in a bowl ricotta, grated cheese and eggs until smooth. Set aside.

1 pound mozzarella, sliced
   thin or grated into tiny
   strips
1/2 cup freshly grated
   Romano cheese

To put lasagne together, place a little sauce on bottom of a large shallow baking pan. Spread 3 cups of rice on bottom of pan; then top with some of the ricotta mixture and tomato sauce; sprinkle with grated cheese and some mozzarella.

Arrange as many successive layers as the dish will hold, ending with cheeses. Dish can be stretched even further by using more rice. Bake at 400° F. for 30 minutes or until bubbly and mozzarella has melted on top. Let stand 10 minutes before serving. Cut into 3-inch by 3-inch squares

and serve with crushed
red pepper.

VARIATIONS
Make lasagne with a
meatless sauce. Substitute
pasta or polenta for rice
in this recipe.

SUGGESTED MENU
Rice Lasagne
Mixed Salad
Italian Garlic Bread

Cassata Cake
Espresso

RICE AND MEATBALLS

Preparation and Cooking Time: 2 hours   **Serves 4–6**

Form tiny meatballs the size of large marbles, fry, and
add to sauce. Serve over rice. Spaghetti and meatball
lovers will be delighted with this variation on their favorite
dish.

INGREDIENTS
To make sauce:
3 tablespoons olive oil
2 garlic cloves, halved
1 2-pound 3-ounce can
   Italian plum tomatoes,
   undrained
1 teaspoon salt
½ teaspoon basil

DIRECTIONS

Heat olive oil in a large
sauce pot and sauté gar-
lic until limp; strain tomatoes through food mill
into pot. Add salt, basil
and black pepper; sim-
mer for 1 hour.

1/8 teaspoon freshly ground
    black pepper

To make meatballs:
1 pound ground beef
2 slices stale white bread,
    grated
2 tablespoons freshly
    grated Romano cheese
1 garlic clove, minced
1 tablespoon minced fresh
    parsley
1/8 teaspoon freshly ground
    black pepper
3 medium eggs

Mix together in a large bowl the ground beef, bread crumbs, grated cheese, garlic, parsley and black pepper. Add eggs one at a time. Mixture should not be too loose or the meatballs will fall apart when fried. Wet hands in cold water before forming meat mixture into tiny balls the size of large marbles. Handle meat mixture gently. *Do not pack meatballs.*

Oil for frying

Heat at least ½ inch of oil in a large skillet. Fry meatballs until crisp and brown on all sides; drain on absorbent paper. Add meatballs to sauce and simmer 1 hour more.

6 cups hot cooked rice
1/4 cup freshly grated
    Parmesan cheese

Remove drained rice to a warmed platter; ladle just enough sauce over the top to coat rice lightly. Sprinkle with cheese, toss, and serve. Meatballs can be mixed with rice or served separately. Pass extra cheese and sauce.

SUGGESTED MENU
Rice and Meatballs
Mixed Green Salad
Italian Garlic Bread

Strawberries in Wine
Espresso

PORCUPINE MEATBALLS IN TOMATO SAUCE

Preparation and Baking Time: 1 hour 30 minutes **Serves 4**

The rice explodes in the meatballs as this casserole cooks.

INGREDIENTS
1 pound ground beef
1/2 cup uncooked rice
1 teaspoon salt
1/8 teaspoon freshly ground
    black pepper

DIRECTIONS
Combine ground beef, uncooked rice, salt and black pepper; mix thoroughly. Form gently into meatballs about 1 inch in diameter. Place in a baking dish. Set aside.

1 tablespoon oil
1 garlic clove, minced
1 small onion, chopped
1/2 green pepper, cored, seeded and chopped (optional)

In a skillet brown onions, garlic and green pepper in olive oil.

2 1/2 cups tomato sauce
1 teaspoon salt
1/4 teaspoon freshly ground
    black pepper

Add tomato sauce, salt and black pepper. Simmer for 10 minutes. Pour over meatballs. Cover and bake at 350° F. for 1 hour or until rice is tender.

SUGGESTED MENU
Porcupine Meatballs in Tomato Sauce
Mashed Potatoes
Peas and Carrots

Peach Pie
Coffee

RICE WITH MEAT SAUCE

Preparation and Cooking Time: 1 hour 30 minutes **Serves 4**

A thick meat sauce is ladled over hot rice.

INGREDIENTS
2 tablespoons olive oil
1 pound ground beef
1 small onion, chopped
1 garlic clove, chopped
1 2-pound 3-ounce can Italian plum tomatoes
1 teaspoon salt
1 tablespoon minced fresh parsley
1/2 teaspoon basil
1/8 teaspoon freshly ground black pepper

4 cups hot cooked rice
1/4 cup freshly grated Parmesan cheese

DIRECTIONS
Heat olive oil in a medium-sized pot; sauté ground beef, onion and garlic, stirring frequently, until lightly browned. Pour off excess fat before straining tomatoes into pot. Season with salt, parsley, basil and black pepper. Simmer for 1 hour.

Ladle just enough sauce over hot rice to cover each grain lightly. Sprinkle with cheese and toss at the table. Pass additional sauce and cheese.

SUGGESTED MENU
Rice with Meat Sauce
Romaine and Tomato
Salad

Sliced Oranges in Wine
Espresso

ETHIOPIAN BEEF AND RICE STEW

Preparation and Cooking Time: 30 minutes   **Serves 4–6**

A ground beef dish, Retfo, which comes from Ethiopia, is too dry to be classified as a stew, although it is usually served with rice.

INGREDIENTS	DIRECTIONS
1 large onion, chopped 1 green pepper, diced 3 tablespoons butter or oil	Sauté onion and pepper in butter in a heavy frying pan until onion is limp and golden.
1½ pounds lean ground beef	Add ground beef and continue frying over moderate heat, stirring and breaking up meat, until it begins to lose its red color.
½ to 1 tablespoon dried crushed red pepper 1½ teaspoons salt ¼ teaspoon freshly ground black pepper	Stir in crushed red pepper, salt and black pepper; continue cooking until meat is well browned. Spoon off fat.
4 cups hot cooked rice.	Serve with rice.

SUGGESTED MENU
*Ethiopian Beef and Rice
Stew*
Tossed Salad

Fresh Fruit Nuts
Coffee

VEAL CUTLETS PAPRIKA

Preparation and Cooking Time: 30 minutes   **Serves 4–6**

This is a light and utterly delicious dish.

INGREDIENTS

DIRECTIONS

2 pounds veal cutlets,
  thinly sliced and
  flattened
Salt
3 tablespoons oil

Sprinkle cutlets with salt; brown lightly in oil in a skillet on both sides. Remove from skillet and reserve.

1 medium onion, chopped
1 teaspoon paprika
½ cup water
1 small green pepper,
  cored, seeded and cut in
  ½-inch strips
½ cup tomatoes, drained

Sauté onion in the same pan. Stir in paprika and water; simmer for 2 minutes. Add meat, green pepper and tomatoes. Simmer for 15 minutes, turning meat once. Sauce should barely cover meat. Cool slightly.

½ cup sour cream, at
  room temperature

Mix a little sauce into sour cream; then pour mixture slowly into sauce, stirring gently. If sauce is too thick, add a little more water. Adjust

116

seasoning if necessary. Simmer for 3 minutes more.

4 cups hot cooked rice

Serve each guest one or two veal cutlets and rice. Spoon sauce over both.

SUGGESTED MENU
Veal Cutlets Paprika
Tossed Green Salad

Baked Apple
Coffee

VEAL AND RICE

Preparation and Cooking Time: 30 minutes   **Serves 4–6**

A bit of Italian sausage adds the seasoning to this veal dish.

INGREDIENTS	DIRECTIONS
6 veal cutlets Salt and freshly ground black pepper to taste 2 tablespoons olive oil	Sprinkle veal with salt and pepper; sauté veal quickly on both sides until light brown in olive oil in a large skillet. Remove from pan. Reserve.
2 links of Italian sausage, cut into ½-inch slices 1 medium onion, sliced thin	In same skillet, fry sausage and onion until well cooked.
2 cups uncooked rice	Stir in rice and sauté until light yellow.

117

1 cup canned tomatoes, undrained	Add tomatoes, parsley and broth; add cutlets and cook, covered, until rice is tender, about 15 minutes.
2 tablespoons minced fresh parsley	
1 quart chicken broth	
½ cup freshly grated Parmesan cheese	Mix with grated cheese and serve at once.

SUGGESTED MENU
Veal with Rice
Sautéed Artichokes
Celery Salad

Ice Cream Cake
Coffee

LAMB WITH RICE

Preparation and Cooking Time: 1 hour 30 minutes   **Serves 4**

An everyday Greek dish.

INGREDIENTS	DIRECTIONS
2 pounds lamb, leg or shoulder cut into bite-sized pieces	Heat butter in a Dutch Oven, add meat and onions. Brown well over moderate heat.
3 tablespoons butter	
2 medium onions, chopped	
1 cup tomato sauce	Add tomato sauce, water, salt and pepper. Bring to a boil; cover and simmer for about 1 hour until meat is almost tender.
1 cup water or bouillion	
Salt and freshly ground black pepper to taste	

1 cup uncooked rice — Add rice and stir well. Bring to a boil again cover and simmer for about 20 minutes or until rice is tender.

SUGGESTED MENU
Lamb with Rice
Greek Tossed Salad

Baklava
Coffee

LAMB CURRY WITH RICE

Preparation and Cooking Time: 1 hour 45 minutes   Serves 4

Curry powder is a mixture of spices which makes a highly spiced stew. The variety of curries is endless.

INGREDIENTS

1½ pounds lamb shoulder or leg, cut in 1-inch cubes

1 teaspoon salt

Freshly ground black pepper to taste

2 tablespoons butter

1 cup hot water

2 tablespoons butter

2 medium onions, chopped

¼ cup flour

2 teaspoons curry powder or to taste

DIRECTIONS

Sprinkle lamb with salt and pepper. Sauté lamb cubes in butter in a large skillet until lightly browned, stirring frequently. Add hot water and simmer covered for 1 hour.

Sauté onions in butter until limp and golden; stir in flour and brown slightly. Add curry powder.

119

2 cups hot beef stock	Gradually add beef stock to flour mixture; cook, stirring constantly, until thickened. Pour sauce over meat and simmer, covered, 30 minutes more or until meat is tender.
2 teaspoons lemon juice 2 tablespoons shredded coconut	Add lemon juice and coconut. Adjust seasoning if necessary.
4 cups hot cooked rice	Arrange border of rice on platter and fill center with curried lamb.

SUGGESTED MENU
Lamb Curry with Rice

Sliced Pineapple and
Cherries
Tea

LAMB PILAF

Preparation and cooking Time: 30 minutes   **Serves 4**

Pilaf or pilau is the Persian or Turkish word that refers to an Oriental dish of rice boiled with meat or fish and spiced.

INGREDIENTS	DIRECTIONS
3 slices bacon, diced 1 small onion, diced	Cook bacon and onion together until bacon is rendered of most of its fat.
½ cup uncooked rice	Stir in rice and cook until brown, about 2 minutes.

1 cup chicken broth	Add chicken broth; simmer until liquid is almost gone.
1 cup diced, cooked lamb 2 cups canned tomatoes, undrained 1 teaspoon salt 1/4 teaspoon freshly ground black pepper 1/2 teaspoon basil 1 bay leaf	Add rest of ingredients; cover and cook 14 minutes or until rice is tender. Remove bay leaf before serving.

SUGGESTED MENU
Lamb Pilaf
Celery and Olive Salad
Garlic Pizza

Pound Cake with Brandied Fruit and Ice Cream
Coffee

LAMB RISOTTO

Preparation and Cooking Time: 1 hour 30 minutes **Serves 4**

Lamb is simmered slowly with tomatoes until fork tender before the rice is added.

INGREDIENTS	DIRECTIONS
4 tablespoons butter 1 small onion, diced	Sauté onion in melted butter in a large skillet.
3/4 pound lamb, cut into 1/2-inch cubes	Add meat and brown on all sides.
1/2 pound fresh tomatoes, cored and cut into	Add tomatoes, salt, pepper and basil; cook

121

quarters, or 1 1-pound can tomatoes, undrained 1 teaspoon salt 1/8 teaspoon freshly ground black pepper 1/2 teaspoon basil	slowly for 45 minutes or until lamb is tender.
1 cup uncooked rice 1 cup meat broth	Add rice and broth; simmer covered for 5 minutes.
2 1/2 cups meat broth	Add rest of broth; simmer, covered, until rice is tender, about 10 minutes longer. Dish should be slightly moist.
1/2 cup freshly grated Parmesan cheese	Stir in cheese and serve at once.

SUGGESTED MENU
Lamb Risotto
Stuffed Green Peppers

Peaches in Wine
Coffee

TURKISH PILAF

Preparation and Cooking Time 30 minutes   Serves 4–6

A versatile dish.

INGREDIENTS
2 pounds boned lamb, cut into 1/2-inch cubes

DIRECTIONS
Brown lamb in butter in a large skillet. Remove

2 tablespoons butter	lamb from pan and reserve.
2 tablespoons butter 1 cup uncooked rice	Add rest of butter and rice; sauté stirring occasionally, until golden.

4 tomatoes, chopped, or
  2 cups drained canned
  tomatoes, chopped
2 cups chicken stock
Salt and freshly ground
  black pepper to taste
	Return meat to pan; add tomatoes, stock and season to taste. Cover and simmer for 20 minutes or until tender.

Yogurt	Serve with yogurt.

SUGGESTED MENU
Turkish Pilaf
Tossed Salad

Watermelon Balls
Coffee

SCALLOPED HAM AND RICE BAKE

Preparation and Baking Time: 45 minutes   **Serves 4–6**

Chopped, hard-boiled eggs are a nice addition.

INGREDIENTS	DIRECTIONS

4 tablespoons butter or
  margarine
4 tablespoons flour
2 cups cream
  evaporated milk
	Heat butter in a saucepan; stir flour into melted butter to make a roux. Slowly add cream, stirring constantly, until thickened.

1-2 cups diced, cooked ham

2 hard-boiled eggs, chopped

½ teaspoon salt

⅛ teaspoon freshly ground black pepper

1 teaspoon Worcestershire sauce

Stir in ham, eggs, salt, black pepper and Worcestershire sauce.

4 cups hot cooked rice

Toss sauce with cooked rice; pour into a shallow casserole.

1 cup buttered bread crumbs

2 tablespoons freshly grated Parmesan cheese

Top with bread crumbs and cheese. Bake at 375° F. for 15–20 minutes until brown and bubbly.

SUGGESTED MENU
Scalloped Ham and Rice Bake
Baked Tomatoes

Applesauce Cake
Coffee

HAM, ASPARAGUS AND RICE SOUFFLE

Preparation and Cooking Time: 1 hour 15 minutes **Serves 4**

Soufflés are marvelous when you have leftovers in the refrigerator.

INGREDIENTS
½ cup diced, cooked asparagus

DIRECTIONS
Place asparagus in bottom of an ungreased 1½-

quart straight-sided casserole. Set aside.

3 tablespoons butter
1/4 cup flour
1 cup warm milk

Melt butter in top of a double boiler; stir in flour until smooth. Add heated milk a little at a time; cook, stirring constantly, over boiling water until smooth and thick.

1/4 cup sharp cheddar cheese, grated
1/2 teaspoon salt
1 teaspoon dry mustard
4 egg yolks, beaten

Add cheese, salt and dry mustard; stir until smooth and creamy. Remove from heat. Stir a little of cheese sauce into beaten egg yolks; slowly stir this mixture into rest of cheese sauce.

4 egg whites, beaten until stiff but not dry
1/2 cup cooked rice
1/4 cup ground cooked ham

Beat egg whites until stiff. Fold egg whites, rice and ham into cheese sauce; pour into casserole. Mixture should not reach the top of the dish. To form a crown, make a shallow path with the edge of a knife about 1 inch from the edge of the rim all the way around.

Preheat oven to 400° F.; bake uncovered for 5 minutes. Lower heat to 375° F. and continue baking for 30 minutes or until golden brown.

125

SUGGESTED MENU
*Ham, Asparagus and
Rice Souffle*

Orange Sherbert
Coffee

BAKED PORK CHOPS WITH RICE

Preparation and Cooking Time: 1 hour 15 minutes

Serves 4–6

Prepare earlier in the day and pop into the oven on a busy day.

INGREDIENTS
1 cup uncooked rice
1 small onion, chopped
2 medium apples, cored
and chopped
3 tablespoons fresh minced
parsley
1 teaspoon salt

6 ½-inch thick pork chops,
trimmed of extra fat
1 tablespoon oil

2 cups chicken stock

DIRECTIONS
Combine rice with onion, apple, parsley and salt. Spread rice mixture on bottom of a baking pan large enough to hold 6 pork chops in a single layer.

Brown pork chops on both sides in hot oil in a skillet. Remove chops and place on top of rice in a single layer.

Add chicken stock to skillet. Bring to a boil, stirring to loosen brown particles from skillet. Pour over pork chops and rice. Cover with foil and

bake in a 350° F. oven
for 1 hour.

SUGGESTED MENU
Baked Pork Chops with
Rice
Beet Salad

Apple Turnovers
Coffee

ARROZ CON PLÁTANOS

Preparation and Cooking Time: 30 minutes   **Serves 4–6**

Latin American countries combine rice with many things
such as sausage and banana.

INGREDIENTS

1 pound link sausage, cut
into ¾-inch slices
½ cup seedless raisins,
soaked
3 bananas, cut into ¾-inch
slices

5 cups cooked rice
Salt and freshly ground
black pepper to taste

DIRECTIONS

Sauté sausage in a large
skillet until well done.
Add bananas and raisins;
stir gently for 3 minutes
or until well coated.

Add cooked rice to skil-
let; toss gently until
heated. Season with salt
and pepper to taste.
Serve immediately.

SUGGESTED MENU
Arroz con Plátanos
Mixed Green Salad
Crescents Butter

Strawberry Shortcake
Coffee

HAM CROQUETTES WITH LEMON SAUCE

Preparation and Cooking Time: 1 hour*   **Serves 4**

A divinely good lemon sauce makes these rice croquettes filled with ham into a first-class eating adventure.

INGREDIENTS	DIRECTIONS
2 teaspoons butter or margarine 2 tablespoons flour 1/2 cup milk	Stir flour into melted butter to make a roux in a saucepan. Add milk; cook, stirring constantly, until sauce thickens.
1/2 teaspoon prepared mustard 1/2 teaspoon lemon juice 1/8 teaspoon freshly ground black pepper	Add mustard, lemon juice and black pepper to mixture. Simmer for 1 minute to blend seasonings, stirring constantly. Remove from heat.
2 cups ground or minced ham 1 cup cooked rice 1/2 medium onion, minced 2 minced teaspoons fresh parsley 1 teaspoon celery salt	Combine sauce with ham, onion, parsley, celery salt and cooked rice; mix well. Cool before shaping into balls or patties.
1 egg, beaten slightly 2 tablespoons water 2 tablespoons freshly grated Parmesan cheese	Mix together egg, water and cheese. Roll each croquette first into bread crumbs; then into egg

*Does not include chilling time.

1 cup dry seasoned bread crumbs	mixture; and back into bread crumbs. Chill.
Oil for frying	Fry croquettes in hot 390° F. oil until golden brown, about 3 minutes. Serve hot with lemon sauce.

To make lemon sauce:
1 chicken bouillon cube
¾ cup hot water
2 eggs, beaten
1½ tablespoons reconstituted lemon juice
½ teaspoon prepared mustard
1 teaspoon sugar

While bouillon cube is dissolving in hot water, beat together eggs and lemon juice. Stir a little hot bouillon into egg mixture; then slowly pour egg mixture into bouillon, stirring constantly. Add other ingredients to saucepan; cook over low heat, stirring constantly, until mixture thickens, about 10 minutes. Serve hot over croquettes.

SUGGESTED MENU
*Ham Croquettes with
Lemon Sauce*
Grated Carrot Salad
with Raisins

Strawberry Sundae
Coffee

RICE WITH SAUSAGE

Preparation and Cooking Time: 45 minutes   **Serves 4**

The risotto is a useful recipe for turning small quantities of meat or seafood into a satisfying meal.

INGREDIENTS	DIRECTIONS
1 pound Italian sausage	Fry sausage in a large skillet until brown and well cooked; cool and slice into ½-inch rings. Remove sausage from skillet; set aside.
1 cup uncooked rice	Pour off all but 3 tablespoons of the fat; brown the rice in fat, stirring frequently.
1 garlic clove, chopped 1 large onion, chopped 3 cups hot chicken or meat stock, approximately ½ cup tomato sauce ½ teaspoon salt ⅛ teaspoon freshly ground black pepper ¼ teaspoon fennel seeds	Add garlic and onion; sauté until onion is limp and golden. Add 1 cup chicken stock, tomato sauce, salt, black pepper and fennel seeds. Cook, stirring constantly, for 10 minutes; add more stock as needed. Add sausage; stop adding liquid when rice is tender with still a little "bite" to each grain. A risotto must be watched closely all the time it is cooking. Stir frequently.

SUGGESTED MENU
Rice with Sausage
Tomato, Cucumber and
  Onion Salad

Ricotta Puffs
Espresso

PORK CHOP SUEY

Preparation and Cooking Time: 45 minutes   Serves 4

The only difference between chop suey and chow mein is
that chow mein is served over crisp Chinese noodles.
Both are inventions of Chinese-Americans in San Fran-
cisco in the nineteenth century.

INGREDIENTS
1/4 cup oil
1 teaspoon salt
1/4 teaspoon freshly ground
    black pepper

DIRECTIONS
Prepare all ingredients
before beginning to cook.
Heat oil sprinkled with
salt and pepper in a
deep, heavy skillet until
almost smoking.

2 cups Chinese cabbage,
    sliced thin
3 cups celery, sliced thin
1 16-ounce can bean
    sprouts, drained, or 2
    cups fresh bean sprouts,
    cleaned

Add Chinese cabbage,
celery, bean sprouts,
water chestnuts and
sugar all at once. Fry,
stirring constantly, for 2
minutes.

1 8-ounce can water
  chestnuts, sliced
2 teaspoons sugar

2 cups chicken broth	Add chicken broth, and cook about 10 minutes. Stir occasionally.
2½ tablespoons cornstarch ¼ cup water ¼ cup soy sauce	Mix cornstarch, water and soy sauce together; add to vegetable mixture. Stir until mixture thickens.
2 cups sliced cooked pork (thin slivers)	Add meat and heat thoroughly.
4 cups hot cooked rice	Serve over hot cooked rice.

SUGGESTED MENU
Chicken Egg-Drop Soup

Pork Chop Suey

Iced Pineapple Rings
Fortune Cookies
Tea

SKILLET PORK CHOPS

Preparation and Cooking Time: 1 hour 10 minutes **Serves 4**

A dinner in one skillet.

INGREDIENTS
4 half-inch shoulder, rib
  or loin pork chops
½ cup flour

DIRECTIONS
Remove excess fat from pork chops. Sprinkle pork chops with flour, salt and

½ teaspoon salt
⅛ teaspoon freshly ground
  black pepper
2 tablespoons oil

pepper; brown in oil in a skillet for 10–15 minutes until chops are browned on both sides. Pour off excess fat and remove chops to dish.

1 cup uncooked rice
1 10½-ounce can onion
  soup
1 can water
1 medium tomato,
  chopped
1 small onion, chopped
½ teaspoon basil

Place rice, onion soup, water, tomato, basil and onion in skillet; top with pork chops in a single layer. Cover and simmer until chops are tender, about 45 minutes. Add more water if necessary.

6 pineapple rings
6 strips of pimiento

Ten minutes before dish is done, place a pineapple ring and a strip of pimiento on each pork chop for an appetizing-looking dish.

SUGGESTED MENU
Skillet Pork Chops
Green Bean Salad

Lemon Pie
Coffee

RICE WITH PORK AND BANANAS

Preparation and Cooking Time: 30 minutes   **Serves 4–6**

A Latin dish that combines pork and bananas sautéed with garlic, and onion with rice. Garnished with slices of hard-boiled egg and green olives.

INGREDIENTS	DIRECTIONS
2 tablespoons oil 2 cups cooked pork, cubed 1 garlic clove, minced 1 small onion, minced	Sauté pork, garlic and onion in oil in a large skillet until onion is limp and golden.
3 bananas, cut into ¾-inch slices 1 tablespoon butter	Add bananas and butter; stir gently for 3 minutes or until well coated.
5 cups cooked rice ¼ cup freshly grated Parmesan cheese Salt and freshly ground black pepper to taste	Add cooked rice and grated cheese to skillet; toss gently until heated. Season with salt and pepper to taste.
3 hard-boiled eggs, sliced ¼ cup pitted green olives	Top with egg slices and olives. Serve immediately.

SUGGESTED MENU
Fresh Fruit Cup

*Rice with Pork and
    Bananas*
Mixed Green Salad

Lime Sherbet Pie
Coffee

Poultry
with
Rice

❧

ARROZ CON POLLO

Chicken with Rice

Preparation and Baking Time: 1 hour 30 minutes **Serves 4**

Chicken baked on a bed of saffron rice is a Spanish dish that has gained tremendous popularity in America.

INGREDIENTS	DIRECTIONS
1 3-pound chicken, cut up 1 teaspoon salt 1/4 teaspoon freshly ground black pepper 1/4 teaspoon paprika 1/3 cup oil	Sprinkle chicken with salt, pepper and paprika. Heat oil in a large skillet until hot; brown chicken on all sides.
1/2 tablespoon lemon juice	Sprinkle browned chicken with lemon juice. Remove chicken from pan and arrange in a shallow 3-quart casserole.
1 medium onion, chopped	Sauté onion and garlic in

1 garlic clove, minced

oil in skillet until limp and golden; sprinkle over top of chicken.

1 cup uncooked rice
1/8 teaspoon saffron
4 cups canned tomatoes, undrained
1 green pepper, cored, seeded and chopped
1 teaspoon salt

Sprinkle rice and saffron on chicken in casserole; add tomatoes with green pepper. Season with salt. Cover tightly and bake at 350° F. for 1 hour.

SUGGESTED MENU
Gaspacho

Arroz con Pollo
Escarole with Oil and
    Vinegar

Fresh Mangoes
Coffee

CHICKEN BREASTS WITH ALMONDS

Preparation and Cooking Time: 45 minutes   **Serves 4**

One of the most excellent of the classical French chicken dishes is **Suprêmes de Volaille Amandine**, sautéed chicken breasts with slivered almonds.

INGREDIENTS
4 small whole chicken breasts, skinned, boned and halved
1 teaspoon salt
1/8 teaspoon freshly ground black pepper
3 tablespoons butter

DIRECTIONS
Sprinkle chicken breasts with salt and pepper. Sauté until brown in butter in a large skillet, turning occasionally. Remove chicken.

138

2 tablespoons butter
1 tablespoon minced onion
1/3 cup slivered almonds

To juices in skillet, add butter, onion and almonds. Cook, stirring occasionally, over low heat until amonds are light brown.

1 teaspoon tomato paste
1 tablespoon flour
1¼ cups chicken broth
1/8 teaspoon tarragon

Blend in tomato paste and flour. Gradually add chicken broth and cook, stirring constantly, until mixture thickens and comes to a boil. Add cooked chicken breasts and tarragon; cover and simmer for 20 minutes.

4 cups hot cooked rice

Serve with rice.

SUGGESTED MENU
Chicken Breasts with Almonds and Rice
Tossed Salad

Chocolate Pie

BAKED CHICKEN WITH ALMOND RICE

Preparation and Cooking Time: 1 hour 15 minutes **Serves 4**

A meal in itself that is really worth making.

INGREDIENTS
1 3-pound chicken, cut up
1/4 cup butter or margarine

DIRECTIONS
Brown chicken on all sides in butter in a large skillet.

2 cups chicken broth

In a separate pan, com-

1 cup uncooked rice
1 cup sliced fresh mushrooms or 1 3-ounce can mushrooms, undrained
1/4 teaspoon salt

bine broth, rice, mushrooms, onion and salt; simmer rapidly for 5 minutes.

1/2 cup slivered almonds

Stir almonds into rice mixture. Pour into a 2-quart casserole; top with browned chicken pieces. Cover and bake for 45 minutes in a 325° F. oven or until done.

SUGGESTED MENU
Baked Chicken with Almond Rice
Tossed Green Salad

Cherry Pie
Coffee

COUNTRY CAPTAIN

Preparation and Cooking Time: 1 hour 30 minutes **Serves 4**

Although this dish sounds as if it had originated down South it comes from India which explains the touch of curry.

INGREDIENTS
1 3-pound chicken, cut up
1/4 cup flour
1/2 cup butter or olive oil

DIRECTIONS
Roll chicken in flour; brown chicken in butter in a large skillet for 15

misutes. Remove from pan and reserve.

1 garlic clove, minced
1 small onion, chopped
1 green pepper, chopped

Add garlic, onion and green pepper to skillet; cook until onion is limp and golden.

2 cups canned tomatoes, undrained
1 cup chicken broth
1½ tablespoons curry powder
½ teaspoon thyme
1 teaspoon salt
¼ teaspoon freshly ground black pepper

Return chicken to skillet; add tomatoes, broth, curry powder, thyme, salt and black pepper; bring to a fast boil. Lower heat; cover and simmer for 15 minutes.

¼ cup raisins or currants
4 cups hot cooked rice
¼ cup toasted, slivered almonds
1 tablespoon minced fresh parsley

Add raisins; simmer, uncovered, for 15 minutes longer. Serve with white rice and sprinkle with almonds and parsley.

VARIATIONS
Prepare this dish earlier in the day. Add raisins and proceed with the rest of the steps when you are ready to serve.

SUGGESTED MENU
Country Captain
with Rice
Tossed Salad
Corn Bread

Iced Pineapple
Cookies
Coffee

CHICKEN CREOLE

Preparation and Cooking Time: 1 hour 15 minutes **Serves 4**

The Creole cooking of Louisiana is one of our regional marvels. Use the leftover gravy from this dish the next day to make a rice dish.

INGREDIENTS

DIRECTIONS

1 3-pound chicken, cut up
1 teaspoon salt
1/8 teaspoon freshly ground black pepper
2 tablespoons butter

Sprinkle chicken with salt and pepper; brown chicken in butter in a Dutch oven. Remove chicken from pan; reserve.

1 cup chopped onions

Sauté onions until limp and golden.

2 tablespoons flour

Push onions to side and stir flour into butter to make a roux.

1 cup canned tomatoes, undrained
2 garlic cloves, minced
1 teaspoon thyme
2 teaspoons minced fresh parsley

Add tomatoes, cloves, thyme and parsley; cook for 10 minutes.

2 bay leaves
1 tablespoon grated lemon rind
1 large green pepper,

Return chicken with bay leaves, lemon rind, green pepper, zucchini, water, salt and pepper to pot;

cored, seeded and diced
1 large zucchini, diced
1 cup boiling water
1½ teaspoons salt
¼ teaspoon freshly ground
   black pepper

4 cups hot cooked rice

cover and cook for 45
minutes or until done.

Serve with rice.

SUGGESTED MENU
*Chicken Creole
   with Rice*
Mixed Salad
Hoe Cakes

Lemon Pie
Coffee

CHICKEN KEBABS

Preparation and Cooking Time: 1 hour 10 minutes

Serves 4–6

A fast and fancy dish if marinated and threaded on skewers in advance.

INGREDIENTS
⅓ cup soy sauce
⅓ cup sherry
2 tablespoons sugar
2 tablespoons chopped
   fresh ginger or 1
   teaspoon ground ginger
3 whole chicken breasts,
   boned, skinned and cut
   into 1½-inch chunks

DIRECTIONS
Combine soy sauce, sherry, sugar and ginger together. Marinate chicken in sauce for 20 minutes.

12 scallions	Thread skewers alternately with chicken and scallions. Broil for 10 minutes or until done.
4 cups hot cooked rice **3 tablespoons butter, at room temperature**	Toss rice with butter. Serve Kebabs on rice.

SUGGESTED MENU
Chicken Kebabs
  with Rice

Tomato, Celery and Black
  Olive Salad
Cherry Tart
Coffee

CHICKEN PIE

Preparation and Cooking Time: 1 hour 30 minutes **Serves 4**

Toasted almonds and sherry make this a chicken pie guests will long remember.

INGREDIENTS
1 3-pound chicken, cut up
Water to cover
½ cup chopped celery
  with leaves
2 tablespoons minced
  onion
1½ teaspoons salt

DIRECTIONS
Combine chicken, water celery, onion and salt in large pot; bring to a boil and cook until chicken is tender. Remove chicken from pot, reserving chicken stock; skin and bone chicken, leaving meat in medium-sized pieces.

¼ cup butter
¼ cup flour
1 cup light cream or milk
1 cup chicken stock
¼ teaspoon dill
¼ teaspoon dry mustard
¼ teaspoon freshly ground
    black pepper
1 3-ounce can mushrooms,
    undrained

Stir flour into melted butter in a skillet to make a roux; add cream, stock, dill, mustard, black pepper and mushrooms. Cook, stirring constantly, until broth is thick and smooth.

½ cup cooked rice
½ cup toasted, slivered
    almonds
2 tablespoons dry sherry

Stir in chicken, rice, almonds and sherry; pour into a 1½-quart baking dish.

Pastry for 1-crust pie

Top with pastry; prick top and crimp edges. Bake for 25–30 minutes in a preheated 400° F. oven.

SUGGESTED MENU
Chicken Pie
Molded Cranberry Salad

Brownies
Coffee

CHICKEN POLYNESIAN

Preparation and Cooking Time: 45 minutes   **Serves 4**

Ginger, curry powder, almonds and coconut are found in this dish.

INGREDIENTS	DIRECTIONS
4 small whole chicken breasts, halved 1 cup sour cream 1 teaspoon salt 1 garlic clove, minced	Marinate chicken in sour cream with salt and garlic for 1 hour. Drain chicken, reserving liquid.
1/4 cup flour 3 tablespoons oil	Roll chicken in flour; brown in hot oil.
1/4 cup water 1/4 cup chopped onion	Add water and onion; cook until tender.
1 tablespoon flour 1/4 teaspoon ginger 1 whole clove 1 1/2 teaspoons curry powder	Blend flour with ginger, clove and curry powder; then mix with reserved sour cream mixture. Add slowly to chicken mixture, stirring constantly until thickened. Discard clove.
4 cups hot cooked rice 2 tablespoons toasted almonds 2 tablespoons shredded coconut	Serve chicken with rice topped with sauce and garnished with almonds and coconut.

SUGGESTED MENU
Chicken Polynesian
Molded Fruit Salad

Orange Sherbet Cookies
Coffee

CHICKEN AND SHRIMP GUMBO

Preparation and Cooking Time: 2 hours   Serves 4–6

Gumbos are a native American dish born of the meeting of French, Spanish and African cookery in Old New Orleans kitchens. Gumbo takes its name from a corruption of the African Bantu word for okra, one of its major ingredients.

INGREDIENTS	DIRECTIONS
½ cup diced salt pork or bacon	Cook salt pork or bacon until rendered of its fat in a large, heavy soup pot.
2 tablespoons butter or margarine 1 3-pound chicken, cut up ¼ cup chopped onion	Add butter to pot; sauté chicken and onion until lightly browned.
2 cups sliced fresh, canned, or frozen (thawed) okra, drained 2 cups canned tomatoes, undrained 1 garlic clove, minced ¼ lemon, thinly sliced 1 bay leaf	Add okra, tomatoes, garlic, lemon slices and bay leaf; bring to a boil.

147

3 cups boiling water 1/2 teaspoon salt 1/4 teaspoon paprika 1/8 teaspoon Tabasco sauce 1 teaspoon Worcestershire sauce	Add boiling water, salt, paprika, Tabasco sauce and Worcestershire sauce; lower heat and simmer, partially covered, for 45 minutes.
1/2 pound fresh shrimp, shelled and deveined, or 1/2 pound frozen shrimp, thawed and drained	Add shrimp and cook for 15 minutes more or until shrimp are pink.
2 tablespoons butter 2 tablespoons flour	Heat butter and blend with flour until smooth; stir mixture slowly into simmering broth; bring to a boil. Remove bay leaf before serving.
4–6 cups hot cooked rice	Serve with rice.

VARIATION
This recipe doubles or triples easily for a large crowd. Add shrimp just before serving.

SUGGESTED MENU
*Chicken and Shrimp
Gumbo with Rice*
Hot Cakes with Butter

Chocolate Chess Pie
Coffee

MANDARIN CHICKEN

Preparation and Cooking Time: 1 hour   **Serves 4**

My friend Mrs. George (Barbara) Davidson gave me this recipe for chicken with orange sauce. It is now a family favorite.

INGREDIENTS
2 1½-pound chickens, cut up
½ teaspoon poultry seasoning
1 teaspoon minced onion flakes
1 teaspoon salt
⅛ teaspoon freshly ground black pepper

2 tablespoons butter
1 tablespoon oil

1 tablespoon flour
1 12-ounce can frozen concentrated orange juice undiluted
2 11-ounce cans mandarin

DIRECTIONS
Sprinkle chicken with poultry seasoning, onion flakes, salt and black pepper.

Heat butter and oil in a large frying pan. Brown both sides of chicken; cook until tender, about 40 minutes. Remove chicken to a warm platter. Drain off all but one tablespoon of fat from pan.

Add flour and orange juice; mix it with the pan scrapings. Then add mandarin oranges and stir for two minutes.

oranges	Sauce will turn a nice brown color.
4 cups hot cooked rice	Serve sauce over chicken and rice.

SUGGESTED MENU
Egg Drop Soup
Mandarin Chicken
with Rice

Kumquats Cookies
Tea

CHICKEN FRICASSEE

Preparation and Cooking Time: 1 hour 15 minutes **Serves 4**

A marvelous fricassee!

INGREDIENTS	DIRECTIONS
1 frying chicken, cut in 8 serving pieces 6 tablespoons butter	Sauté chicken until lightly browned on all sides. Cover pan and cook at low heat for 10 minutes, turning once.
Salt Freshly ground black pepper 2 tablespoons flour	Sprinkle with salt, pepper and flour; cover and cook for 5 minutes, turning once. Flour will start to brown. Remove chicken to a casserole. Set aside.
2 cups stock	Pour stock into pan and scrape up any bits stuck to the bottom. Pour over

chicken; cover and simmer for 30 minutes or until done.

2 tablespoons butter
2 tablespoons minced
  shallots or scallions
1 cup sliced mushrooms
1 tablespoon chopped
  fresh parsley

Meanwhile, sauté shallots or scallions in butter until limp. Add mushrooms and sauté lightly. Stir in parsley and cook for 1 minute. After chicken has been cooking 15 minutes, add mushroom mixture to pan.

½ cup sour cream, at
  room temperature

When chicken is done, remove pot from heat and let it cool. Skim off excess grease. Stir a little sauce into sour cream; then slowly pour it back into the sauce.

4 cups hot cooked rice

Simmer for 2 minutes more before serving over hot rice.

SUGGESTED MENU
Chicken Fricassee
  with Rice
Sautéed Tomatoes

Cherry Pie
Coffee

MEXICAN CHICKEN FRICASSEE

Preparation and Cooking Time: I hour 20 minutes **Serves 4**

Highly seasoned with onion, green pepper, garlic and chili powder, this Mexican dish is a fresh, peppery version of classic stewed chicken. Raisins and black olives add an unusual note.

INGREDIENTS

1 3-pound chicken, cut up
½ cup flour
½ cup oil

DIRECTIONS

Roll chicken pieces in flour; fry in hot oil in a large frying pan until brown on all sides. Remove chicken from pan; reserve.

1 medium onion, sliced
1 small green pepper, cored, seeded and chopped
2 garlic cloves, minced

Sauté onion, green pepper and garlic in the same pan until onion is limp and golden.

4 tablespoons tomato paste
1½ cups water
1 teaspoon chili powder
2 teaspoons salt

Add tomato paste, water, chili powder and salt; bring to a boil. Lower heat and simmer rapidly for 5 minutes. Return chicken to pan; cover and simmer for 45 minutes or until chicken is tender.

4 tablespoons raisins

Add raisins and olives;

½ cut pitted black olives, sliced — toss and simmer for 10 minutes more.

4 cups hot cooked rice — Serve with rice.

SUGGESTED MENU
— *Mexican Chicken Fricasse with Rice*
Sliced Tomatoes and Cucumbers

Ice Cream Pie
Coffee

CHICKEN PAPRIKA

Preparation and Cooking Time: 1 hour   Serves 4

An Hungarian classic.

INGREDIENTS
1 3-pound chicken, cut up
1½ teaspoons salt
¼ teaspoon freshly ground black pepper
1 teaspoon paprika
¼ cup flour
2 tablespoons oil

DIRECTIONS
Sprinkle chicken with salt, pepper and paprika. Roll chicken in flour. Heat oil in a large skillet and brown chicken on all sides.

1 small onion, diced
¾ cup chicken broth
2 teaspoons lemon juice

Add onions, chicken broth and lemon juice; cook, covered, over low heat for about 40 minutes until chicken is tender. Skim off excess fat.

153

3 tablespoons flour 1 cup sour cream	Blend flour into half the sour cream; stir into chicken. Stir in remaining sour cream; simmer for 5 minutes. Do not boil.
4 cups hot cooked rice	Serve with rice.

SUGGESTED MENU
Chicken Paprika
with Rice
Buttered Peas

Peach Pastry
Coffee

CHICKEN STROGANOFF

Preparation and Cooking Time: 40 minutes   **Serves 4**

Nobody will complain about dinner when you serve this dish.

INGREDIENTS

DIRECTIONS

4 whole chicken breasts, boned, skinned and halved 1½ teaspoons salt ¼ cup butter	Sprinkle chicken breasts with salt; sauté quickly in hot butter in a large skillet.
1 medium onion, diced ½ pound mushrooms, sliced	Add onion and mushrooms; cook for 2 minutes longer.
¼ cup sherry ½ teaspoon thyme	Add sherry and thyme; reduce heat and cook, covered, for 5 minutes.

1 tablespoon flour 2 tablespoons water	Blend flour and water together. Add to skillet and cook, stirring constantly, until thickened.
1 cup sour cream 1½ teaspoons paprika	Stir in sour cream and paprika; heat but do not boil.
4 cups hot cooked rice	Serve with rice.

SUGGESTED MENU
*Chicken Stroganoff
with Rice*
Buttered Asparagus

Fruit Compote
Cookies
Coffee

AFRICAN CHICKEN AND RICE STEW

Preparation and Cooking Time: 1 hour 30 minutes

Serves 4–6

The best known of one-dish stews in West Africa is Jollof Rice, common all along the coast. The rice is cooked right in the stew itself.

INGREDIENTS	DIRECTIONS
1 3-pound chicken, cut up Salt and freshly ground black pepper to taste 4 tablespoons peanut oil	Season chicken with salt and pepper; brown in hot oil in a stewing pan. Remove chicken and reserve.
6 onions, diced ½ tablespoon crushed red pepper	In same pan, sauté onions and red pepper.

1 8-ounce can tomato sauce	Add tomato sauce and tomatoes. When vegetables are cooked, add browned chicken and 1 cup water. Simmer over low heat until chicken is tender, about 45 minutes.
3 cups canned tomatoes, undrained	
1 cup water	
1 chicken bouillon cube	Dissolve bouillon cube in 1½ cups boiling water; add to stew and bring to a fast boil.
1½ cups boiling water	
1 cup rice	Add rice and stir well. Cover, reduce heat, and simmer until rice is tender.
1½ cups water	

SUGGESTED MENU
*African Chicken and Rice
    Stew*
Rolls

Fresh Fruit Nuts
Coffee

CHICKEN AND VEAL RISOTTO

Preparation and Cooking Time: 30 minutes   **Serves 4**

An extremely pretty rice dish. The white wine enhances the flavor of both the chicken and veal.

INGREDIENTS
2 tablespoons butter
2 chicken breasts, boned,

DIRECTIONS
Sauté in melted butter in a large skillet the chicken,

skinned and cut into
  1-inch cubes
1 chicken liver, diced
2 veal cutlets, cut into
  1-inch squares
1 small onion, diced
1 carrot, grated
1 stalk of celery with
  leaves, diced

onion, carrot, chicken liver, veal and celery until vegetables are limp and golden, about 10 minutes.

1 cup uncooked rice
½ cup dry white wine
1 teaspoon salt
⅛ teaspoon freshly ground
  black pepper

Add rice and sauté until golden in color. Add wine, salt and black pepper; simmer until wine is almost absorbed.

3 cups hot chicken stock

Add chicken stock; cover and simmer until rice is tender, about 10 minutes. Add more stock if necessary. Dish should be moist.

SUGGESTED MENU
Stuffed Artichoke

Chicken and Veal Risotto
Sliced Tomatoes

Apple Tart
Coffee

CHICKEN STROGANOFF

Preparation and Cooking Time: 30 minutes   **Serves 4**

Stroganoff was named after P. Stroganoff, a Nineteenth-century Russian count and diplomat. Sautéed chicken breasts and fresh mushrooms are simmered in a delicate sour cream sauce.

INGREDIENTS

DIRECTIONS

4 whole chicken breasts, skinned, boned and halved
1½ teaspoons salt
¼ cup butter

Sprinkle chicken with salt; sauté quickly in hot butter in a large skillet until tender and browned on both sides.

1 medium onion, finely chopped
½ pound fresh mushrooms, cleaned and sliced

Add onion and mushrooms; sauté until onion is limp and golden, stirring constantly.

1 tablespoon flour
2 tablespoons water

Blend flour and water; add to skillet all at once; cook, stirring constantly, until thickened.

1 cup sour cream
1½ teaspoons paprika

Stir in sour cream and paprika; heat thoroughly but do not boil.

4 cups hot cooked rice

Serve with rice.

SUGGESTED MENU
Borsch

Chicken Stroganoff
    with Rice
Buttered Broccoli

Fruit Pastries
Tea

CHICKEN AND SAUSAGE RISOTTO

Preparation and Cooking Time: Serves 4

Freshly grated Parmesan cheese turns this dish into something special.

INGREDIENTS	DIRECTIONS
½ pound sausage links, cut into 1-inch pieces	Brown sausage in a skillet. Remove and reserve.
1 3-pound chicken, cut up	Brown chicken in drippings. Remove chicken and reserve. Discard fat.
2 cups canned tomatoes, mashed 1 cup water ¾ cup uncooked rice 1 garlic clove, minced 1 medium onion, chopped 1 teaspoon salt ⅛ teaspoon freshly ground black pepper 1 bay leaf	Stir in tomatoes, water, rice, garlic, onion, salt, black pepper and bay leaf. Return sausage and chicken to pan; simmer covered for 40 minutes or until tender.
¼ cup freshly grated Parmesan cheese	Sprinkle with cheese before serving.

SUGGESTED MENU
*Chicken and Sausage
Risotto*
Lettuce, Avocado and
Black Olive Salad

Raspberry Sherbert
Butter Cookies
Coffee

THAILAND CHICKEN WITH RICE

Preparation and Cooking Time: 30 minutes   **Serves 4**

Lime juice is an important ingredient.

INGREDIENTS
6 half chicken breasts, skinned, boned and cut into 1/4-inch strips
4 tablespoons oil

2 tablespoons chopped onion
1/2 cup sliced fresh mushrooms or 1 3-ounce can mushrooms, drained
1 teaspoon ginger
1 garlic clove, minced
Pinch of coriander
1 teaspoon salt
1/8 teaspoon freshly ground black pepper

1 1/2 tablespoons soy sauce

DIRECTIONS
Lightly brown chicken strips in sizzling oil in a large skillet.

Add onion, mushrooms, garlic, ginger, coriander, salt and pepper. Reduce heat, cover pan, and cook for 10 minutes.

Combine soy sauce, vine-

1 tablespoon cider vinegar
Juice of 1 lime or lemon
1 teaspoon sugar

gar, lime juice and sugar.
Add to chicken; bring to
a boil and simmer for 5
minutes more.

4 cups hot cooked rice

Serve with rice.

SUGGESTED MENU
Thailand Chicken with Rice
Stir-fried Broccoli

Iced Pineapple Cookies
Tea

CHICKEN TANDOOR

Preparation and Cooking Time: 1 hour 5 minutes* **Serves 4**

This authentic recipe comes from Pakistan.
Serve with the traditional curry accompaniments.

INGREDIENTS
2 1½-pound chickens, halved
2 large onions, chopped
2 green peppers, diced
2 tomatoes, chopped
2 teaspoons salt
1 tablespoon curry powder
1 tablespoon coriander
1 tablespoon ground cumin
1 teaspoon turmeric
½ teaspoon cinnamon
½ teaspoon garlic powder

DIRECTIONS
Place chicken in a shallow baking pan. Sprinkle with onion, green pepper, tomato, salt, curry powder, coriander, ground cumin, turmeric, cinnamon, garlic powder and black pepper. Pour melted butter over the top. Mix with chicken. Cover and marinate in refrigerator several hours

*Does not include marinating time.

½ teaspoon freshly ground
    black pepper to taste
¼ pound butter, melted

or overnight.

2 cups water

Mix in water and bake in
375° F. oven for 1 hour
or until chicken is tender.

4 cups hot cooked rice

Serve with rice and any
of the traditional curry
accompaniments.

Suggested curry
   accompaniments:
Chopped peanuts
Sieved hard-boiled eggs
Yogurt or sour cream
Grated coconut
Grated onion
Chutney

SUGGESTED MENU
Chicken Tandoor
   with Rice
Curry Accompaniments

Strawberry Ice Cream
Coconut Cookies
Coffee

PAELLA VALENCIAGO

Preparation and Cooking Time: 1 hour   **Serves 4–6**

Paella is a casserole which must always be based on rice, but in Spain the other ingredients vary according to the available food. Chicken and shrimp are coupled with artichokes and green peas in this version.

INGREDIENTS	DIRECTIONS
1 3-pound chicken, cut into 2-inch pieces ¼ cup olive oil	Have the butcher cut the chicken into small pieces unless you have a cleaver which will cut through the bones. Brown chicken in olive oil in a paella pan or large skillet until chicken is tender.
2 medium tomatoes, quartered ½ cup chopped green pepper 1 small onion, chopped 2 garlic cloves, minced	Add tomato, green pepper, onion and garlic to pan; sauté until onion is transparent, about 5 minutes, stirring constantly.
1½ cups uncooked rice 1 teaspoon saffron	Stir into pan or skillet rice and saffron; cook over medium heat, stirring constantly, for 5 minutes.
4 cups chicken broth	Add chicken broth; bring to a boil; cover and cook

over medium heat for 10 minutes.

½ pound shrimps, cleaned and deveined
1 teaspoon salt
¼ teaspoon paprika
1 cup frozen green peas, thawed and drained
1 package frozen artichokes, parboiled, or 2 cups canned artichokes, drained

Add shrimps, salt, paprika, green peas and artichokes; cook 10 minutes more until rice is tender and shrimps are pink, stirring gently once or twice. If necessary, add more broth.

This dish should be dry and the liquid absorbed, so add additional broth as necessary.

VARIATION
This dish can be assembled and baked in the oven.

SUGGESTED MENU
Paella Valenciago
Tossed Green Salad

Custard Pie
Coffee

JAMBALAYA

Preparation and Cooking Time: 1 hour **Serves 4**

Jambalaya (derived from the Spanish word **jamon** meaning ham) was introduced to New Orleans by the Spanish in the late 1700s. It is considered one of the classic Creole dishes.

INGREDIENTS

1/4 cup diced salt pork, or
    3 slices bacon, diced,
    or 2 tablespoons butter

1 large green pepper,
    cored, seeded and diced
1 large onion, chopped
1 garlic clove, minced

1 1/2 cups diced, cooked
    ham
2 1/2 cups canned
    tomatoes, undrained
1/2 cup water
1 tablespoon minced fresh
    parsley or 1 teaspoon
    dried parsley
1/2 teaspoon thyme
1 teaspoon salt
1/8 teaspoon freshly ground
    black pepper
Pinch of cayenne pepper
    (optional)

3/4 cup uncooked rice
2 cups fresh shrimp,

DIRECTIONS

Cook salt pork or bacon until rendered of its fat in a large skillet.

Add green pepper, onion and garlic, and sauté until onion is limp and golden.

Add ham, tomatoes, water, parsley, thyme, salt and black pepper. Bring to a boil.

Add rice and shrimp to boiling broth; reduce

165

shelled, deveined and washed, or 2 cups frozen shrimp, thawed and drained

heat and simmer, covered, over low heat 30 minutes or ustil rice is tender and most of the liquid has been absorbed. Add more water if dish becomes too dry.

SUGGESTED MENU
Fresh Fruit Cup

Jambalaya
Chilled Green Beans
    with Oil and Vinegar

Lemon Sherbet
Coffee

GERMAN CHICKEN FRICASSEE

Preparation and Cooking Time: 1 hour   Serves 4

Germans cook dried fruits with meat or poultry and add a bit of spice. Here's a recipe for chicken in a gently spiced fruit sauce.

INGREDIENTS
1/4 cup flour
1 teaspoon salt
Freshly ground black
    pepper to taste
1 3-pound chicken, cut up

1/4 cup oil

DIRECTIONS
Combine flour, salt and pepper. Coat chicken pieces with flour mixture, reserving leftover flour mixture to thicken the sauce.

Brown chicken on all sides in hot oil in a Dutch oven.

1 cup pitted prunes
1 cup chicken broth
1 stick cinnamon
1 1-inch long piece of
  fresh ginger
1½ teaspoons brown sugar

Add prunes, chicken broth, cinnamon, fresh ginger and brown sugar. Bring to a boil. Reduce heat and cover. Simmer for 40 minutes or until chicken is tender.

2 tablespoons water
4 cups hot cooked rice

Combine reserved flour mixture with water. Remove cooked chicken and prunes to serving platter and keep warm. Bring sauce to a boil; slowly stir in flour mixture. Simmer for 2 minutes, stirring constantly. Spoon sauce over chicken and hot cooked rice.

SUGGESTED MENU
German Chicken Fricassee with Rice
Butter Broccoli

Apple Cake
Coffee

CHICKEN-RICE PIE

Preparation and Cooking Time: 45 minutes   **Serves 4–6**

This pie has a rice crust.

INGREDIENTS
To make rice crust:
4 cups cooked rice

DIRECTIONS
Mix together rice, eggs, melted butter, salt, black

2 eggs, beaten
1/2 cup melted butter
1 teaspoon salt
Freshly ground black
    pepper to taste
1/4 cup freshly grated
    Parmesan cheese

pepper and cheese. Reserve 1 cup of mixture for top of pie. Pat remaining rice mixture over bottom and on sides of a 10-inch-deep pie plate. Set aside.

To make filling:
3 tablespoons butter
1/4 cup flour
2 cups chicken broth

Melt butter; add flour and blend. Add chicken broth and cook over medium heat, stirring constantly, until mixture comes to a boil and is thickened.

1 tablespoon parsley
1 teaspoon salt
1/4 teaspoon freshly ground
    black pepper
3 cups diced cooked
    chicken

Add parsley, salt, pepper and chicken.

1/2 cup freshly grated
    Parmesan cheese

Pour into rice-lined pie plate. Sprinkle with reserved cup of rice mixture and grated cheese.

Bake at 350° F. for 20 minutes. Serve hot.

SUGGESTED MENU
Chicken-Rice Pie
Peas and Carrots

Chocolate Cake
Coffee

JAPANESE CHICKEN AND MUSHROOMS WITH RICE

Preparation and Cooking Time: 30 minutes   Serves 4–6

The Japanese name for this dish—**Oyako Domburi**—means mother and child. The chicken is carried on top of the rice.

INGREDIENTS	DIRECTIONS
1 large chicken breast, skinned, boned and cut into thin shreds 4 large fresh mushrooms, sliced 4 small scallions with tops, sliced	Prepare chicken breasts, mushrooms and scallions.
½ cup fish or chicken stock ¼ cup soy sauce ¼ cup sake	Bring fish stock, soy sauce and sake to a boil; add chicken, mushrooms and scallions. Cook over low heat until chicken and vegetables are tender.
5 eggs, beaten	Stir in eggs; cook until eggs are set, stirring gently once.
4 cups hot cooked rice	Serve on rice, and with soy sauce.

SUGGESTED MENU
*Japanese Chicken and
Mushrooms with Rice*

Tangerine Jello with
Whipped Cream
Tea

CHICKEN AND RICE WITH MORNAY SAUCE

Preparation and Cooking Time: 20 minutes   Serves 4–6

A Mornay sauce is made with Swiss cheese and heavy cream.

INGREDIENTS	DIRECTIONS
To make Mornay Sauce: 4 tablespoons butter 4 tablespoons flour	Melt butter in a saucepan over medium heat. Add flour and cook, stirring constantly, until golden and bubbly.
1½ cups chicken stock	Gradually add chicken stock; cook, stirring constantly, until you have a smooth sauce.
½ cup grated Swiss cheese ½ cup heavy cream Salt and freshly ground black pepper to taste	Add cheese and cream; heat but do not boil. Season with salt and pepper.
3 tablespoons butter 3 shallots, finely chopped 1 pound fresh mushrooms, sliced	Heat butter in a skillet; sauté mushrooms and shallots until tender.
4 cups cubed, cooked	Add the cooked chicken

chicken	and sauce; simmer until hot.
6 cups cooked rice	Serve chicken sauce on a platter surrounded by a border of cooked rice.

SUGGESTED MENU
*Chicken and Rice with
  Mornay Sauce*
Buttered Peas

Peaches in Wine
Coffee

CHICKEN LIVERS AND RICE

Preparation and Cooking Time: 30 minutes   **Serves 4-6**

This dish will make chicken livers extremely popular—even with the kids!

INGREDIENTS	DIRECTIONS
2 tablespoons butter 8 chicken livers Salt and freshly ground black pepper to taste	Heat butter in a skillet and sauté chicken livers. Season with salt and black pepper.
1/4 cup oil 1 large onion, minced 1 cup uncooked rice	Heat oil in a heavy skillet; sauté onion until limp and golden. Add rice and sauté, stirring constantly, until transparent.
3 cups chicken broth	Mix together broth, to-

⅔ cup tomato sauce
1½ tablespoons hot
  mustard
3 tablespoons minced
  fresh parsley

mato sauce mustard and parsley. Add to rice mixture; simmer, covered, for 15 minutes.

Add chicken livers and mix thoroughly. Cover and cook until all liquid had been absorbed and rice is tender. Add a little more broth if necessary. Adjust seasoning if necessary.

SUGGESTED MENU
Chicken Livers and Rice
Broiled Tomatoes

Lemon Pie
Coffee

GREEK CHICKEN PILAF

Preparation and Cooking Time: 1 hour   Serves 4

Cinnamon and cloves add new flavor. Served with sour cream.

INGREDIENTS
4 chicken breasts
4 tablespoons butter
Salt and freshly ground
  black pepper to taste

1 medium onion, finely
  chopped

DIRECTIONS
Brown chicken in butter with salt and black pepper.

Add onion, tomatoes, water, cinnamon and

172

1 cup canned tomatoes	clove; cover and simmer
1½ cups water	for 30 minutes.
Dash of cinnamon	
Dash of clove	

| ⅔ cup uncooked rice | Add rice and stir to mix evenly. Cover and simmer for 20 minutes more or until rice is done, adding more water if necessary. |

| 1 cup sour cream | Serve with a bowl of sour cream. |

SUGGESTED MENU
Greek Chicken Pilaf
Greek Tossed Salad with
Feta

Honey Cake
Coffee

CHICKEN LIVER AND RICE CASSEROLE

Preparation and Baking Time: 45 minutes   **Serves 4**

Prepare in advance so you can pop it in the oven the minute you come in the door at night. So easy.

INGREDIENTS
2 tablespoons butter or margarine
1 pound chicken livers, cut in half

DIRECTIONS
Brown chicken livers in butter until cooked in a large skillet.

1 3-ounce can mushrooms, undrained
1 10½-ounce can mushroom soup
⅓ cup milk
2 tablespoons white wine
Dash of freshly ground black pepper

Add mushrooms and liquid, mushroom soup, milk, white wine and black pepper. Simmer, stirring occasionally, until hot and smooth.

3 cups cooked rice

Mix in rice and pour into a 2-quart casserole.

¼ cup toasted slivered almonds

Sprinkle top with almonds. Bake at 350° F. for 30 minutes.

SUGGESTED MENU
Chicken Liver and Rice Casserole
Buttered Broccoli
Tomato Salad

Peach Shortcake
Coffee

CHICKEN LIVER RISOTTO

Preparation and Cooking Time: 30 minutes   **Serves 4**

A different way to prepare chicken livers which is nothing short of terrific!

INGREDIENTS
2 tablespoons butter
2 tablespoons olive oil
1 small onion, diced
1 garlic clove, minced

DIRECTIONS
Sauté onion and garlic in olive oil and butter in a large skillet until limp and golden.

1 cup uncooked rice 1 cup hot chicken broth	Stir in rice until golden. Add stock; cover and simmer until almost absorbed, about 5 minutes.
2½ cups hot chicken stock	Add rest of stock; cover and simmer for 10 minutes more until rice is tender.
3 tablespoons butter 1 small onion, diced ½ pound chicken livers, quartered 1 cup sliced fresh mushrooms Strip of lemon peel Salt and freshly ground black pepper to taste 2 tablespoons chicken stock 2 tablespoons white wine	Meanwhile, in a separate skillet, sauté onion in butter until limp; add chicken livers and mushrooms. Sauté until lightly browned. Add lemon peel; season with salt and pepper to taste. Add stock and white wine; cover and simmer until cooked, about 10 minutes. Remove lemon peel and add to cooked rice.
¼ cup freshly grated Parmesan cheese 1 tablespoon butter	Toss with grated cheese and butter before serving.

SUGGESTED MENU
Fresh Fruit Cup

Chicken Liver Risotto
Tossed Green Salad

Cherry Cheesecake
Coffee

CHICKEN LIVERS IN WHITE WINE

Preparation and Cooking Time: 45 minutes   **Serves 4**

Fresh mushrooms, onions and chicken livers are sautéed in butter; then simmered gently until done in a delicate white wine sauce.

INGREDIENTS
1/4 cup butter or margarine
1 medium onion, minced
1 cup sliced fresh
   mushrooms
1 pound chicken livers

DIRECTIONS
Sauté onion, mushrooms and chicken livers in butter in a large frying pan until onions are limp and golden. Remove chicken livers from pan; reserve.

2 tablespoons flour
1 cup chicken broth
1/2 cup white wine
1 teaspoon salt
1/8 teaspoon freshly ground
   black pepper

Add flour to pan drippings and blend well. Stir in chicken broth, wine, salt and black pepper until mixture is thickened and smooth, about 10 minutes. Return chicken livers to pan; simmer for 10 minutes more or until done.

4 cups hot cooked rice

Serve with rice.

VARIATION
Almond rice is especially good with this dish.

SUGGESTED MENU
Chicken Livers in White

Wine with Rice
Buttered Peas

Fresh Peach Parfait

CORNISH HENS WITH RICE STUFFING

Preparation and Cooking Time: 2 hours 30 minutes **Serves 4**

Diced pork flavors the rice stuffing of this splendid company dish.

INGREDIENTS	DIRECTIONS
1 tablespoon oil 1/4 pound pork, diced	Brown pork in oil in a large skillet. Remove pork from pan; reserve.
1 small onion, finely chopped 1 garlic clove, minced	Sauté onion and garlic in same skillet until limp and golden; remove from pan and reserve with pork.
1 cup uncooked rice 1 tablespoon oil	Add rice and oil to skillet; sauté until rice turns golden. Stir frequently.
2 cups hot chicken broth Salt and freshly ground black pepper to taste	Add hot chicken broth, pork, onion and garlic to rice mixture; cover and simmer for 20 minutes or until rice is tender. Season to taste with salt and black pepper.
4 1-pound Cornish hens	Stuff Cornish hens with rice mixture. Place in greased baking pan; bake,

177

uncovered, at 375° F. for about 1½ hours. Baste occasionally.

To make gravy:
1½ cups chicken broth
⅛ cup sherry
1 cup canned mushrooms

Add to juices from Cornish hens the chicken broth, sherry and mushrooms; simmer for 15 minutes.

1 tablespoon cornstarch
Salt and freshly ground
black pepper to taste

Stir cornstarch into a little of mixture separately; then add to pan, stirring constantly, over low heat until thickened. Season to taste and serve separately with Cornish hens.

SUGGESTED MENU
Onion Soup

Cornish Hens with Rice Stuffing
Buttered Green Beans
Waldorf Salad
Cranberry-Orange Relish
Rolls Butter

Trifle
Coffee

TURKEY PILAF

Preparation and Cooking Time: 30 minutes   **Serves 4**

Toasted slivered almonds make this turkey-rice pilaf special.

INGREDIENTS
3 tablespoons butter
1 small onion, chopped
1 cup uncooked rice

2 cups chicken broth
1/2 teaspoon salt
1/8 teaspoon freshly ground
    black pepper

2 cups diced, cooked
    turkey
1/2 cup toasted slivered
    almonds
1/2 cup seedless raisins
    (optional)

DIRECTIONS
Sauté onion in butter in a skillet until limp and golden. Add rice and stir until rice is golden.

Add broth, salt and pepper; cover and simmer until rice is tender and dry. Add more broth if necessary.

Add turkey and heat until hot. Sprinkle with almonds and raisins if desired before serving.

SUGGESTED MENU
Turkey Pilaf
Broiled Tomatoes
Beet and Onion Salad

Peach Pie
Coffee

Vegetables
with
Rice

❧

VEGETABLE RISOTTO

Preparation and Cooking Time: 30 minutes   **Serves 4**

Whatever vegetable is in season—e.g., zucchini, potatoes, mushrooms—can be used in this superbly simple risotto.

INGREDIENTS
2 tablespoons butter
1/2 cup diced bacon
1 small onion, diced
1 garlic clove, minced

1 pound zucchini, potatoes, mushrooms or any seasonal vegetable, cleaned and coarsely chopped
1 tablespoon minced fresh parsley
Salt and freshly ground black pepper to taste

1 cup uncooked rice
3 1/2 cups hot meat stock

DIRECTIONS
Sauté onion and garlic and render bacon of fat in a large skillet.

Add vegetable, parsley, salt and pepper; sauté until lightly browned.

Add rice and stir for 1 minute to brown lightly before adding hot stock. Simmer for about 14 minutes or until rice is tender, stirring occasionally. Dish should be quite dry.

½ cup freshly grated Parmesan cheese

Toss rice mixture with grated cheese; let stand for 3–4 minutes before serving.

ASPARAGUS RISOTTO

Preparation and Cooking Time: 30 minutes Serves 4

Crisp, fresh vegetables are best in this dish.

INGREDIENTS | DIRECTIONS
6 tablespoons butter
1 pound fresh asparagus, cleaned and cut into 2-inch pieces, or 2 boxes frozen asparagus, thawed and drained
1 small onion, thinly sliced

Sauté vegetables in melted butter until onion is limp and golden.

1 cup uncooked rice

Stir in rice until coated and golden in color, about 1 minute.

1 cup boiling beef or chicken stock

Stir in boiling stock; cover and simmer for 3 minutes or until liquid is absorbed.

2½ cups boiling beef or chicken stock

Gradually add 1 cup of stock at a time until rice is tender, about 10–12

minutes. Rice should be
on the dry side.

¾ cup freshly grated Parmesan cheese I tablespoon butter	Stir in butter and grated cheese; let stand 3–4 minutes before serving to blend flavors.

PUMPKIN RISOTTO

Preparation and Cooking Time: I hour   **Serves 6**

An unusual use for pumpkin in this country, but not so in Italy.

INGREDIENTS	DIRECTIONS
I small pumpkin	Peel pumpkin and discard seeds. Cut into small pieces.
3 tablespoons butter 3 tablespoons olive oil I small onion I cup boiling water Salt to taste	Heat butter and oil in a large pan; sauté onion until limp and golden. Add pumpkin and boiling water; season to taste with salt and continue cooking until pumpkin is tender, about 15 minutes.
2 cups uncooked rice 5–6 cups boiling water	Stir rice into mixture gently; continue cooking until liquid is absorbed. Add another cup of water and as rice dries out continue in this man-

185

ner until rice is tender, about 20 minutes.

3 tablespoons butter 1/2 cup freshly grated Parmesan cheese	Stir in butter and cheese gently; cover pan and allow to lay 2–3 minutes to blend the flavors. Serve hot with additional grated cheese.

HUNGARIAN STRING BEANS AND RICE

Preparation and Cooking Time: 1 hour 30 minutes **Serves 4**

An exceptional, nourishing side dish of braised green beans cooked with rice. Sour cream is added at the end. Perfect with steak or lamb chops.

INGREDIENTS	DIRECTIONS
1/4 cup rice Water Salt	Parboil rice in salted water for 10 minutes; drain and reserve.
1/4 cup oil 1 medium onion, chopped 1 tablespoon chopped fresh parsley 1 teaspoon paprika Salt to taste 1 pound string beans, cleaned and cut into 1-inch lengths	Heat oil in a skillet; sauté onion until limp and golden. Stir in parsley, paprika, salt and string beans. Cook them in the fat for about 5 minutes, stirring constantly. Do not let them brown.
1 teaspoon vinegar 2 cups water	Mix vinegar in water and pour over beans. Cover and simmer for 45 minutes. Add rice and

cook for another 15 minutes or until beans are tender. Cool.

½ cup sour cream, at room temperature

Mix some of bean mixture into sour cream; then slowly pour it back into pot. Simmer for 2 minutes and serve hot.

JAPANESE RED BEANS AND RICE

Preparation and Cooking Time: 2 hours 30 minutes

Serves 4–6

This combination of red beans and rice is a favorite dish of the Japanese. **Mochigome,** a glutinous-type rice, is used with **azuki,** Japanese red beans. This recipe calls for regular rice and red kidney beans.

INGREDIENTS
1 cup dried red kidney beans, washed
Water to cover

DIRECTIONS
Put washed beans and water in a pot; bring to a boil. Remove from heat and let stand 1 hour; drain.

1 teaspoon salt
Water to cover

Cover with water; add salt. Cover and cook over low heat for 1 hour or until beans are tender. Drain, reserving water.

1 cup rice, washed
1 teaspoon salt

Put rice, salt and 1½ cups of water in which beans were cooked in a saucepan. Bring to a boil;

187

add cooked beans. Cover pan and bring to a boil. Reduce heat and cook over very low heat 20 minutes.

3 tablespoons sake
3 tablespoons toasted sesame seeds

Add sake; mix lightly. Cook over low heat until dry, about 5 minutes. Serve cold sprinkled with toasted sesame seeds.

CABBAGE WITH RICE

Preparation and Cooking Time: 30 minutes   **Serves 4**

Especially tasty with pork or sausage.

INGREDIENTS
1 2-pound Savoy cabbage, cleaned, cored and cut into quarters

DIRECTIONS
Prepare cabbage by removing old leaves and washing; then remove core and cut into quarters. Set aside.

1/4 pound salt pork or slab bacon, cut into 1/2-inch cubes
2 garlic cloves, minced
1/2 cup water
1/8 teaspoon freshly ground black pepper

Fry salt pork or bacon cubes in a large skillet until almost done but not yet crisp; add garlic and sauté until limp. Remove from heat and carefully add water. Place cabbage into skillet; season with black pepper; cover and cook slowly for 20 minutes or until vegetables are tender.

4 cups hot cooked rice

Add drained cooked rice to cabbage mixture when done. Allow to sit on turned-off burner for 10 minutes before serving.

RICE AND PEAS

Preparation and Cooking Time: 40 minutes   Serves 4

This tasty dish of rice and peas makes a fine accompaniment for simple meals.

INGREDIENTS
3 tablespoons olive oil
1 medium onion, chopped
1 8-ounce can tomato sauce
½ teaspoon salt
⅛ teaspoon freshly ground black pepper

1 medium can peas undrained

4 cups hot cooked rice
3 tablespoons freshly grated Parmesan cheese

DIRECTIONS
Heat olive oil in a large saucepan; sauté onion until limp and golden. Add tomato sauce, salt and black pepper; simmer rapidly until sauce cooks down to a thick, dry consistency.

Add undrained peas to sauce; cook slowly for 15 minutes longer.

Add hot cooked rice to sauce; turn off heat; sprinkle with grated cheese; let rest for 5 minutes before serving.

VARIATION
Substitute spaghetti for rice.

189

CHICK PEAS AND RICE

Preparation and Cooking Time: 30 minutes* **Serves 4**

Serve with fish or pork.

INGREDIENTS
3 tablespoons olive oil
2 large onions, chopped

2 cups hot cooked rice
1 20-ounce can chick peas, drained
1/2 teaspoon salt
1/8 teaspoon freshly ground black pepper

DIRECTIONS
Heat olive oil in a medium skillet and sauté onions until limp and golden.

Add rice, chick peas, salt and black pepper. Cook over low heat, stirring occasionally, until mixture becomes dry like fried rice.

VARIATION
Cooked lentils can be substituted for chick peas.

*Includes cooking time for rice.

CURRIED PEAS AND RICE

Preparation and Cooking Time: 35 minutes   **Serves 4**

Chopped pickles and fresh mint are added to this dish from India at the last minute.

INGREDIENTS
3 tablespoons butter
2 medium onions, finely chopped
1 garlic clove, minced
1 tablespoon curry powder
1 bay leaf
2 cloves

DIRECTIONS
Heat butter in a large skillet; sprinkle onion and garlic in pan with curry powder. Add bay leaf and cloves; sauté mixture until onion is limp and golden.

1½ cups uncooked rice
Water

Add rice and stir until rice is a light yellow. Add enough water to cover mixture by ½ inch (2–3) cups. Bring to a boil; reduce heat and cook rice, covered, for 16 minutes.

1 large package frozen peas, thawed and drained
Salt and freshly ground black pepper to taste

Add drained peas to mixture; stir and season with salt and pepper. Cook until peas are done to taste, adding more water if necessary. Dish should have a creamy consistency.

2 tablespoons chopped
fresh mint
2 tablespoons chopped
celery
2 small sweet-sour gherkins,
chopped

Stir in mint, celery and
pickles. Serve hot.

BAKED OKRA AND RICE

Preparation and Cooking Time: 1 hour   Serves 4–6

Young, tender okra is a necessity in this dish.

INGREDIENTS
3 cups young okra, cut
into thin slices
1/4 cup uncooked rice
4 cups canned tomatoes,
undrained
1 teaspoon salt
Freshly ground black
pepper to taste
Curry powder
Butter

DIRECTIONS
Sprinkle bottom of
greased baking dish with
a tablespoon of rice.
Cover with a layer of
okra; then with a layer of
tomatoes. Season with
salt, pepper, curry pow-
der and dot with butter.
Repeat the layers until
ingredients are used up.
Cover and bake in a 325°
F. oven for 45 minutes.
Uncover and bake for 10
minutes more to brown
top.

GREEK SPINACH AND RICE

Preparation and Cooking Time: 40 minutes   **Serves 4**

Mint flavors this dish while tomato adds extra color.

INGREDIENTS
1 large onion, finely chopped
1/2 cup olive oil
2 tomatoes, sliced

1 pound fresh spinach, washed, or 2 packages frozen spinach, thawed and drained
1 cup uncooked rice
1 teaspoon chopped fresh mint
Salt and freshly ground black pepper to taste
2 cups water

DIRECTIONS
Sauté onions in oil until soft. Add tomatoes and simmer until sauce thickens slightly.

Add spinach, rice, mint, salt, pepper and water as needed. Cover and simmer until rice is tender, about 20 minutes.

TOMATO, OKRA AND RICE CASSEROLE

Preparation and Cooking Time: 1 hour 15 minutes
Serves 6–8

Serve with poultry or meat.

INGREDIENTS
1/4 cup diced salt pork

DIRECTIONS
Cook salt pork until crisp; remove from skillet.

1 small onion, chopped
1 cup sliced okra

Cook onion and okra in bacon fat until onion is limp and golden.

1 cup uncooked rice
2 16-ounce cans tomatoes
1 teaspoon salt
1/8 teaspoon freshly ground black pepper
Tabasco sauce to taste
1/2 cup water
1 tablespoon minced fresh parsley

Add rice, tomatoes, salt, pepper, Tabasco sauce, water and parsley. Bring to a boil. Pour into a greased casserole. Bake at 350° F. for 1 hour or until rice is tender.

CARROT RICE RING

Preparation and Cooking Time: 35 minutes   **Serves 4–6**

A pretty, tasty combination.

INGREDIENTS
3 large carrots, shredded
Boiling water
Salt

DIRECTIONS
Briefly parboil shredded carrots in boiling salted water. Drain thoroughly.

1 tablespoon chopped onion
1 1/2 cups cooked rice
1 egg, beaten
Salt and freshly ground black pepper to taste
1 cup freshly grated Parmesan cheese

Mix carrots with onion, rice, egg, salt, pepper and grated cheese. Pour into buttered ring mold; bake in 350° F. oven for 30 minutes.

2 cups cooked buttered peas

Unmold on platter and serve with hot buttered peas in center.

MEXICAN RICE WITH ARTICHOKE HEARTS

Preparation and Cooking Time: 45 minutes   **Serves 6–8**

A black bean base for this rice dish makes it extra special.

INGREDIENTS

DIRECTIONS

I can black beans, undrained
Chicken stock

Put black beans in blender with enough chicken stock to make 2½ cups. Blend until mixture is smooth and watery, not thick.

I cup uncooked rice
Warm water to cover

Soak rice in warm water for about 10 minutes. Rinse in cold water. Drain.

3 tablespoons oil
I garlic clove, minced
I small onion, minced

Heat oil and sauté rice; stir in a minced onion and garlic clove until rice is golden.

⅓ cup tomatoe purée
I tablespoon chopped fresh parsley
Salt and freshly ground black pepper to taste

Stir in tomato pureé and simmer for 3 minutes. Add bean liquid, parsley, salt and pepper to taste. Mix thoroughly. Cover and simmer for 20 minutes or until rice is done. Add more broth if necessary.

1 cup canned peas 6 canned artichokes hearts 1/4 cup canned pimientos, cut into strips	Add peas, artichoke hearts and pimientos.
1/3 cup toasted almonds 1/3 cup ham, cut in strips	When done, turn into a hot dish and garnish with toasted almonds and ham strips.

RICE RING WITH AVOCADO SAUCE

Preparation and Cooking Time: 1 hour   **Serves 4–6**

Your favorite rice is molded and topped with guacamole sauce.

INGREDIENTS
To make rice:
1/3 cup oil
1 onion, minced
1 cup uncooked rice

DIRECTIONS
Heat the oil; sauté onion until limp and golden. Add rice and stir until transparent.

2 cups hot chicken broth
2 tablespoons minced
fresh parsley
Salt and freshly ground
black pepper to taste

Add broth, parsley, salt and pepper. Simmer, covered, for 20 minutes.

2/3 cup freshly grated
Parmesan cheese

Add cheese; stir well and cook until all liquid is absorbed. Pack rice into a well-buttered ring mold. Place mold in a pan of warm water and cook in a 350 °F. oven for about 30 minutes. When hot, unmold on a platter and cover with guacamole sauce.

To make guacamole (avocado sauce):
2 medium very ripe avocados
2 medium tomatoes
1 small onion, grated fine
1 tablespoon chili powder or to taste
1 tablespoon olive oil
1 teaspoon lime juice
1 teaspoon lemon juice
Dash of paprika
1 teaspoon salt
Freshly ground black pepper to taste

Mash avocados with a fork. Add the other ingredients and stir into a paste that has texture and is not too smooth.

If made ahead of time, wrap dish with cellophane so it will not darken.

HOPPIN JOHN

Preparation and Cooking Time: 35 minutes   Serves 6–8

An easy version of this Southern favorite which features black-eyed peas, salt pork and rice.

INGREDIENTS
¼ pound salt pork or smoked bacon, diced

DIRECTIONS
Fry salt pork or bacon until brown and crisp in a large skillet.

1 package frozen black-eyed peas, parboiled
3 cups cooked rice
1 teaspoon salt

Add peas, rice, salt, black pepper and crushed red pepper or Tabasco to taste. Heat, stirring occasionally, until flavors are

197

1/4 teaspoon freshly ground
    black pepper
Crushed red pepper or
    Tabasco to taste

blended,   about   10
minutes.

RICE AND MUSHROOMS

Preparation and Cooking Time: 30 minutes   **Serves 4**

Fresh mushrooms and white wine make this rice dish notable company fare.

INGREDIENTS
2 tablespoons olive oil
2 tablespoons butter
1 small onion, diced

1 garlic clove, minced
1 cup uncooked rice

1 cup dry white wine

2 1/2 cups boiling chicken
    stock

1/2 pound fresh mushrooms,
    cleaned and sliced
3 tablespoons butter
1 tablespoon fresh minced
    parsley

DIRECTIONS
Sauté onion in butter and oil until limp and golden in a big skillet.

Stir in rice and garlic until it becomes light yellow, about 1 minute.

Stir in white wine; cover and simmer 3 minutes or until wine is absorbed.

Gradually add stock, a little at a time, until rice is tender, about 10–12 minutes. Cover skillet and simmer slowly. Rice will be on the dry side when finished.

While rice is cooking, sauté mushrooms in a separate skillet sprinkled with parsley, salt and pepper until tender. Stir

Salt and freshly ground black pepper to taste	mushrooms into a rice skillet when rice is almost done. Cover and finish cooking.
1 tablespoon butter 1/4 cup freshly grated Parmesan cheese	Toss with grated cheese and butter and let stand 3–4 minutes before serving. Serve with additional cheese if desired.

SKILLET RICE AND ZUCCHINI

Preparation and Cooking Time: 30 minutes   Serves 4

Pretty and so good! Sautéed zucchini and onion tossed with rice is flavored with freshly grated Parmesan cheese, black pepper and Tabasco sauce.

INGREDIENTS	DIRECTIONS
1/4 cup butter or olive oil 1 medium onion, chopped 2 medium zucchini, sliced	Sauté onion and zucchini in butter or olive oil in a large skillet until both are tender, stirring occasionally.
2 cups cooked rice 1/2 teaspoon Tabasco sauce 1/4 teaspoon freshly ground black pepper	Add cooked rice, Tabasco sauce and black pepper; stir until blended.
1 scallion with green top, minced 1/4 cup chopped fresh parsley	Toss scallion, parsley and grated cheese with rice mixture. Serve immediately.

199

1 cup freshly grated
  Parmesan cheese

HUNGARIAN STUFFED CABBAGE

Preparation and Cooking Time: 3 hours   **Serves 6**

This dish is probably the best-known Hungarian specialty in this country.
Stuffed cabbage is one of the glories of Hungarian cooking.

INGREDIENTS

DIRECTIONS

6 cups fresh sauerkraut

Simmer sauerkraut for 1 hour in a large covered kettle.

12 large, unbroken
   cabbage leaves
½ cup water

Meanwhile steam cabbage leaves in water until slightly wilted. Drain and cool.

1 medium onion, chopped
3 tablespoons lard
2 pounds lean, ground
  pork, or beef, or a
  mixture of both

Brown onion in the fat. Add pork and brown it.

1 cup cooked rice
2 eggs
1 teaspoon salt
1 teaspoon paprika
¼ teaspoon marjoram
Pinch of freshly ground
  black pepper

Stir in rice, eggs, salt, paprika, marjoram and pepper. Spread this meat mixture onto cabbage leaves. Roll up and tuck in the ends. Remove half sauerkraut from kettle. Place cabbage rolls in kettle upon the other half; then cover with remaining sauerkraut. Simmer gently for 2 hours.

1 cup sour cream

When ready to serve, stir sour cream into the sauerkraut juices.

SUGGESTED MENU
Hungarian Stuffed Cabbage

Peach Melba
Coffee

GREEK STUFFED CABBAGE

Preparation and Cooking Time: 1 hour   Serves 6–8

My friend Mrs. Joe (Chris) LaRosa shared her mother's superb recipe for this famous stuffed cabbage served in a delicate egg-lemon sauce.

INGREDIENTS
1 3-pound cabbage
Water to cover

DIRECTIONS
Cut core out of cabbage with a "V" cut. Put cabbage in a large pot in enough water to cover; boil gently until you can separate leaves with a knife and a fork. Color of cabbage will change to translucent. Drain cabbage leaves, reserving juice for later, and cut large leaves in half before stuffing.

To make stuffing:

1½ pounds ground beef 2 medium onions 2 tablespoons fresh chopped parsley 4 large tomatoes, chopped, or 1 17-ounce can tomatoes, drained 2 small zucchini (optional) 1 teaspoon salt or to taste 3 tablespoons butter, melted 1 tablespoon oil ¼ teaspoon black pepper ¾ cup uncooked rice, washed	Place beef in a large mixing bowl. Grate onions into bowl so you won't lose the onion juice. Mix meat, onions, parsley, mint, tomatoes, salt, butter, oil, black pepper and rice together gently.

To stuff cabbage:

Take enough of the meat mixture to make a tiny hot dog and place on cabbage leaf on the wider edge. Roll top; tuck in sides and continue rolling. Cut up "core" parts of cabbage and place on bottom of a large pot. Put stuffed cabbage in circles on top; continue to layer stuffed cabbage until done. Put a plate on top.

1 16-ounce can chicken broth
Water
2–3 bouillon cubes

Add chicken broth and enough water from cabbage to cover cabbage rolls. Add 2 or 3 bouillon cubes depending upon amount in pot. Cook for 30–35 minutes.

**To make Avgolemono
(egg-lemon) sauce:**
2 eggs
Juice of 1 lemon or 2–3
ounces lemon juice

Beat eggs and lemon juice together. Add a bit of the liquid from cabbage to warm the egg mixture, stirring constantly. Add stirring to cabbage. When mixed, remove from heat and serve at once.

SUGGESTED MENU
Greek Stuffed Cabbage
Italian, French or Greek
Bread

Baked Apple
Coffee

SHRIMP-STUFFED PEPPERS

Preparation and Cooking Time: 45 minutes   **Serves 4**

Vegetables stuffed with a shrimp-rice stuffing are an exciting new dish everyone in the family will like.

INGREDIENTS
4 large green peppers,
   tops removed and
   seeded

2 cups chopped cooked
   shrimps, or any leftover
   seafood or meat
1/2 cup minced onion
2 tablespoons butter

DIRECTIONS
Simmer green peppers in boiling water for 5 minutes; drain. Set aside.

Combine shrimp, onion, butter, Worcestershire sauce, salt, black pepper, rice and tomato sauce; fill peppers with stuffing.

203

1 teaspoon Worcestershire
  sauce
1 teaspoon salt
1/4 teaspoon freshly ground
  black pepper
1½ cups cooked rice
1 cup tomato sauce

2/3 cup buttered bread
  crumbs

Top with bread crumbs;
bake in a casserole con-
taining half an inch of
water for 25–30 minutes
in a 375° F. oven.

SUGGESTED MENU
Shrimp-Stuffed Peppers
Chicory with Anchovy
  Salad
Cheese Pastry Straws

Strawberry Ice Cream
Coffee

LAMB-STUFFED PEPPERS

Preparation and Cooking Time: 1 hour 30 minutes **Serves 4**

Capers and black olives are the secret ingredients.

INGREDIENTS
2 tablespoons olive oil
1–2 cups coarsely ground,
  cooked lamb
1 small onion, minced

1 egg, beaten
4 tablespoons freshly

DIRECTIONS
Sauté lamb and onion in
olive oil in a large skillet
until brown; remove from
heat.

Mix lamb and onion to-
gether with egg, cheese,

grated Parmesan cheese
1 teaspoon salt
1/4 teaspoon freshly ground black pepper
1/8 teaspoon oregano
1/4 cup bread crumbs
1 tablespoon capers, drained
2 tablespoons black olives, sliced
1 cup cooked rice

salt, black pepper, oregano, bread crumbs, capers, black olives and rice; stuff green peppers with mixture. Place in a baking pan with just enough water to cover the bottom; bake for 15 minutes in a preheated 400° F. oven.

1 8-ounce can tomato sauce

Pour tomato sauce over top of peppers; bake at 350° F. for 45 minutes or until peppers are done. Baste occasionally with sauce. Let stand for 5 minutes after removal from oven before serving.

SUGGESTED MENU
Lamb-Stuffed Peppers
Celery and Tomato Salad

Pecan Ice Cream Cookies
Coffee

TURKEY, CRAB AND RICE STUFFED SQUASH

Preparation and Cooking Time: 1 hour   **Serves 4**

Turkey and crab meat is mixed with a sour cream dressing.

INGREDIENTS
2 medium acorn squash, cut in half lengthwise and seeded

2 cups sour cream
1/2 cup diced cooked crab meat
3/4 cup diced cooked turkey
1 cup cooked rice
1 tablespoon tarragon vinegar
1/2 teaspoon salt
Butter

1/2 cup shredded Swiss cheese

DIRECTIONS
Place squash cut side down on baking sheet; bake for 35–40 minutes at 350° F. until tender.

Meanwhile, combine sour cream crab meat, turkey, rice and vinegar. Turn up cut side of squash; sprinkle with salt and dot with butter. Fill with sour cream mixture; bake 15 minutes more or until hot.

Just before it is done, sprinkle with Swiss cheese. Melt before serving.

SUGGESTED MENU
Turkey, Crab and Rice Stuffed Squash
Tossed Green Salad

Chocolate Pudding
Coffee

PORK AND RICE STUFFED ACORN SQUASH

Preparation and Cooking Time: 1 hour 15 minutes **Serves 4**

Stuffed with a basic sausage and rice stuffing.

INGREDIENTS	DIRECTIONS
2 acorn squash, halved and seeded Water	Place squash with cut side down in a baking pan with an inch of water; cover and bake at 400° F. for 45 minutes or until tender.
2 cups coarsely ground pork or crumbled sausage 1 medium onion, minced 2 tablespoons oil	Meanwhile, sauté pork or sausage and onion in oil in a skillet until well browned.
2 cups cooked rice 1 teaspoon salt 1/8 teaspoon freshly ground black pepper 2 tablespoons freshly grated Parmesan cheese	Mix rice, salt, black pepper and cheese with sausage. Fill centers of cooked squash with the mixture; bake uncovered for 30 minutes at 375° F.

SUGGESTED MENU
*Pork and Rice Stuffed
Acorn Squash*

Fruit Salad

Coffee

RICE-STUFFED PUMPKIN

Preparation and Cooking Time: 1 hour 45 minutes

Serves 4–6

A moist, flavorful ground beef and rice filling baked in a pumpkin or squash shell.

INGREDIENTS

DIRECTIONS

1 3-pound pie pumpkin
1 teaspoon salt
1 teaspoon dry mustard

Cut lid out of pumpkin; remove seeds. Prick inside cavity with fork. Rub inside with salt and mustard. Set aside.

1 tablespoon oil
2 small onions, chopped
1 pound ground beef

Cook onion, garlic, ground beef in a skillet until lightly browned. Remove from heat.

2 large eggs, beaten
1 cup cooked rice
1/4 teaspoon freshly ground black pepper
1 teaspoon salt
1 tablespoon butter, at room temperature

Add eggs, rice, pepper, salt and butter. Stuff pumpkin or squash with mixture. Replace lid.

1 cup water

Place stuffed pumpkin in shallow pan with water. Bake in a 350° F. oven for 1½ hours or until pumpkin or squash is tender. Add water if necessary.

SUGGESTED MENU
Rice-Stuffed Pumpkin
Rolls

Strawberry Ice Cream Pie
Coffee

GREEK STUFFED GRAPEVINE LEAVES

Dolmadakia

Preparation and Cooking Time: 1 hour 15 minutes

Makes **2 dozen**

An excellent appetizer.

INGREDIENTS

2 tablespoons olive oil
2 medium onions, finely chopped
1 teaspoon salt

1/2 cup uncooked rice
4 tablespoons olive oil
1 teaspoon chopped fresh mint
1 teaspoon chopped fresh dill
1/4 cup chopped fresh parsley
1 large bunch scallions including top, chopped
Salt and freshly ground

DIRECTIONS

Put olive oil, onions and salt in pan; cover and steam over low heat until onions are limp and golden, about 5 minutes.

Add rice, olive oil, mint, dill, parsley, scallions, salt and pepper and half the lemon juice; mix thoroughly.

black pepper to taste
Juice of 1 lemon

1 8-ounce jar grapevine leaves

Wash grapevine leaves thoroughly to remove all brine. Cut large leaves in half. Place 1 tablespoon filling on underside of leaf. Starting at base, fold over, and fold in sides, rolling tightly toward point.

Put torn leaves on bottom of a greased casserole. Arrange rolls in circles, making more than one layer if necessary.

2 tablespoons olive oil
Water to cover

Add olive oil and rest of lemon juice. Cover with a heavy plate to keep rolls from opening when rice grows. Cover pot and simmer for 20 minutes over low heat. Add more boiling water at this point to cover and cook 25 minutes longer. Serve cold, sprinkled with lemon juice.

GREEK STUFFED GRAPEVINE LEAVES WITH AVGOLEMONO SAUCE

Preparation and Cooking Time: 1 hour 30 minutes

Serves 4–6

Grapevine leaves are stuffed with rice and ground beef.

INGREDIENTS
¾ pound ground beef
2 medium onions, chopped
⅔ cup uncooked rice
Salt and freshly ground
   black pepper to taste
1 teaspoon chopped fresh
   mint or ½ teaspoon
   dried mint
⅛ cup chopped fresh
   parsley
⅔ cup water

1 12-ounce jar grapevine
   leaves

DIRECTIONS
Combine meat, onions, rice, salt pepper, mint and parsley. Add water and mix well.

Drain brine from jar of grapevine leaves; remove leaves and wash well to remove all traces of brine. Put a tablespoon of meat and rice mixture in center of a leaf and roll leaf tightly, folding edges over and rolling toward point of leaf. Put torn leaves on bottom of a greased casserole. Arrange rolls in circles, making more than one layer if necessary.

2–3 bouillon cubes
Water to cover
1 tablespoon butter

Dissolve bouillon cubes in enough water to cover rolls; add to casserole and dot with butter. Cover with a heavy plate to keep rolls from opening when rice grows. Cover casserole and steam over low heat 1 hour. Add more water if necessary. Serve with Avgolemono Sauce.

To make Avgolemono
(egg-lemon) sauce:
2 eggs
Juice of 1 lemon or
2–3 ounces lemon juice

Beat eggs and lemon juice together. Add a bit of the liquid from casserole to warm the egg mixture, stirring constantly. Add, stirring, to broth. When mixed, remove from heat and serve at once.
If necessary to reheat, leave uncovered while warming very slowly, so egg sauce will not curdle.

GREEK STUFFED TOMATOES

Preparation and Cooking Time: 45 minutes   **Serves 6**

Serve with broiled lamb chops or steak.

INGREDIENTS

6 medium firm tomatoes
Salt
Sugar

DIRECTIONS

Wash tomatoes, cut off top, and scoop out pulp. Save caps. Sprinkle inside of tomatoes with salt and sugar.

1 large onion, grated
1/4 cup olive oil

Sauté onion in 1/4 cup olive oil until limp and golden.

1/4 cup fresh chopped parsley
1/4 cup chopped fresh dill
1/4 cup raisins
1/4 cup pignolia nuts
1/2 cup uncooked rice
1/4 cup olive oil
Salt and freshly ground black pepper to taste

Mix onions, parsley, dill, raisins, nuts, rice and 1/4 cup olive oil together. Season with salt and black pepper. Fill tomatoes with this mixture.

1/2 cup water
2 tablespoons olive oil

Cover with reserved tomato caps and place in a casserole with water. Sprinkle with olive oil. Cover with a heavy plate. Simmer for about 30 minutes or until rice is done. Serve cold.

STUFFED PEPPERS WITH RICE AND MEAT

Preparation and Cooking Time: I hour 20 minutes **Serves 4**

Serve for lunch with mashed potatoes or baked macaroni.

INGREDIENTS

4 medium green peppers, washed and dried

DIRECTIONS

Cut stem off and enough of the top of the pepper to remove seeds and membranes. Set aside.

1 tablespoon olive oil
1/2 pound ground beef
1 cup cooked rice
1 large egg, beaten
1/4 cup freshly grated Parmesan cheese
1/2 small onion, minced
1/8 teaspoon freshly ground black pepper
Pinch of oregano
2 tablespoons dry unseasoned bread crumbs
Water

Heat olive oil in a large skillet; sauté beef until slightly brown. Cool. Mix into skillet, rice, egg, grated cheese, onion, black pepper, oregano and bread crumbs. Stuff peppers. Place stuffed peppers in a baking pan large enough to hold peppers in upright position; add just enough water to cover bottom of pan. Bake in a 350° F. oven for 15 minutes.

1 8-ounce can tomato sauce

Pour tomato sauce over peppers; continue to bake for 45 minutes or until peppers are tender. Baste occasionally. Let stand 10 minutes before serving.

SUGGESTED MENU
*Stuffed Peppers with
Rice and Meat*
Celery and Anchovy
Salad

Cheesecake with Straw-
berries
Coffee

ANCHOVY AND RICE-STUFFED TOMATOES

Preparation and Cooking Time: 1 hour 15 minutes **Serves 6**

The addition of anchovy and capers turns this dish into something special. Serve with broiled chicken or baked lamb.

INGREDIENTS	DIRECTIONS
6 large firm tomatoes Salt	Slice off tops and reserve them to use as "lids." Scoop out pulp and reserve. Sprinkle tomato shells with salt.
2 tablespoons olive oil 1 garlic clove, minced 1/2 cup uncooked rice	Heat olive oil in a skillet; sauté garlic and rice until rice is translucent.
1/2 cup chicken stock or water Salt and freshly ground black pepper to taste	Add tomato pulp, stock, salt, pepper, parsley and basil. Cook over low heat for 10 minutes. Cool.

215

1 tablespoon fresh minced
    parsley
1/2 teaspoon basil

3 anchovy filets, minced 3 teaspoons capers 3 tablespoons freshly grated Parmesan cheese	Stir in anchovy filets, capers and grated cheese. Stuff tomatoes; arrange in an oiled baking dish. Sprinkle with olive oil; cover and bake in a 350° F. oven for about 45 minutes, removing cover for the last 10 minutes. Serve hot or cold.

DOLMAS

Turkish Stuffed Vegetables

Preparation and Cooking Time: 1 hour   **Serves 6**

Your choice of vegetables are stuffed with seasoned lamb and rice.

INGREDIENTS

To make filling:

1 pound ground lamb
1 medium onion, chopped
1/4 cup uncooked rice
1 1/2 cups canned whole
    tomatoes, drained
1/2 cup minced fresh
    parsley (save stems)
1 teaspoon salt

DIRECTIONS

Combine lamb, onion, rice, tomatoes, parsley, salt and pepper, and dill. Mix well.

216

Freshly ground black
   pepper to taste
¼ cup chopped fresh dill
   (save stems)

Suggested Vegetables:
3 medium zucchinis,
   scraped and washed
3 medium green peppers
3 medium firm tomatoes

Prepare vegetables. Scrape and wash zucchinis. Cut off stems and save to be used as lids. Scoop out insides and discard pulp. Prepare peppers and tomatoes by cutting off tops. Reserve to be used as lids. Scoop out and discard insides. Fill vegetable shells with meat mixture a little at a time. When full, replace stem ends as lids.

Put reserved dill and parsley stems on rack in heavy baking pan. Place stuffed vegetables on top. Use two pans if necessary. Dot with butter. Add half an inch of water to bottom of pan.

Butter
Water

Place a heavy plate on top to keep vegetables compact when rice swells. Cook in a 350° oven for about 45 minutes or until done.

RICE AND SPINACH CROQUETTES

Preparation and Cooking Time: 15 minutes*   **Serves 4**

Croquettes are a wonderful way to use up leftovers.

INGREDIENTS

1 cup cooked rice
3 cups chopped cooked spinach
3 eggs, beaten
1/2 teaspoon salt
1/4 cup freshly grated Parmesan cheese
1/8 teaspoon freshly ground black pepper

DIRECTIONS

Mix together rice, spinach, eggs, salt, cheese and black pepper. Form into small balls the size of golf balls.

Dry seasoned bread crumbs

Roll balls in bread crumbs. These can be made ahead and refrigerated.

Oil for frying

Drop rice balls into hot 375° F. oil, a few at a time, and fry until golden, about 3 minutes. Keep fried croquettes hot in oven until served.

*Does not include chilling time.

PIROGEN

Mushroom and Rice Pastries

Preparation and Baking Time: 45 minutes*   **Makes 24**

A delicious first course or main dish.

INGREDIENTS
To make dough:
2 cups water
½ cup margarine or oil

2 packages dry yeast
2 teaspoons salt
4 tablespoons sugar

2 eggs, beaten
3–4 cups flour

DIRECTIONS
Heat water and margarine in a saucepan until water is hot and margarine begins to melt.

Mix yeast with salt, sugar and 4 cups flour. Add water and margarine and mix well.

Beat in eggs. Gradually beat in enough of remaining flour to make a soft dough. Turn out onto lightly floured surface; knead dough until smooth and elastic. Place in a greased bowl; turn, to grease top of dough; cover and let rise in a warm place until double in bulk.

To make filling:
¼ cup butter or margarine   Heat butter in a large

*Does not include time for dough to rise.

1 cup chopped celery 1 cup minced onion 1 garlic clove, minced 2 6-ounce cans chopped mushrooms, drained 1 teaspoon salt 1/4 teaspoon freshly ground black pepper 1/4 teaspoon nutmeg	skillet. Add celery, onion, garlic, mushrooms, salt, pepper and nutmeg; cook for 5 minutes.
1 bay leaf 1/4 cup dry white wine	Add bay leaf and wine; simmer, uncovered, for 10 minutes, until most of liquid evaporates.
1 cup cooked rice	Mix in cooked rice. Remove bay leaf. Heat.
	To make Pirogen: Punch down and divide dough into 24 parts. Flatten each ball of dough. Place 2 tablespoons of filling in the middle and pull dough around it, pinching edges all around with fingers until filling is sealed in the dough. Place on floured waxed paper, cover with towels and place in a warm place until double.
Oil for frying	Fry in hot oil until golden brown, turning once. Drain on absorbent paper. Serve hot.

Salads

LEFTOVER RICE SALAD

Preparation and Cooking Time: 5 minutes   **Serves 4**

A basic recipe which allows you to use whatever you have left over.

INGREDIENTS
3 cups cold cooked rice
1 cup leftover meat or poultry, sliced in thin strips
2 tablespoons minced green pepper
3 scallions with tops, chopped

2 tablespoons lemon juice
6 tablespoons olive oil
1/2 teaspoon salt
Freshly ground black pepper to taste

DIRECTIONS
Combine rice, meat, green pepper and scallions in a bowl; toss lightly with a fork.

Mix together lemon juice, olive oil, salt and pepper. Pour over rice and meat mixture. Toss and serve.

RICE AND VEGETABLE SALAD

Preparation Time: 5 minutes   **Serves 4–6**

Americans are only now discovering the joys of rice salads.

INGREDIENTS
3–4 cups cold cooked rice
1 heart of celery, chopped
   or celeriac
1 cup sliced bottled
   artichoke hearts in oil
1 cup sliced bottled
   mushrooms in oil
1 7¾-ounce can tuna fish,
   drained and flaked
2 medium tomatoes,
   peeled and diced
½ cup sliced black olives
¼ cup chopped anchovies
¼ cup olive oil
½ teaspoon capers
1 red Italian onion, thinly
   sliced
¼ teaspoon freshly ground
   black pepper or to taste
Salt to taste

DIRECTIONS
Rice should be firm and dry, the grains separate. Toss rice together with celery artichokes mushrooms, tuna fish, tomatoes, olives, anchovies, capers, onions, olive oil and black pepper. Season with salt if necessary. Arrange on a serving dish.

Garnish with lemon wedges, hard-boiled eggs, tomato and onion rings, and parsley if desired.

LEMON RICE SALAD

Preparation Time: 10 minutes*   **Serves 4**

A cool, piquant salad which brings out the best in veal, lamb or chicken in the summertime.

INGREDIENTS
2 cups cooked rice
1 tablespoon olive oil
1 teaspoon chopped fresh chives
1 teaspoon minced fresh parsley
½ teaspoon dill
Juice of 1 lemon

DIRECTIONS
Combine all the ingredients; toss and chill at least 1 hour before serving.

*Does not include chilling time.

EGG-RICE SALAD

Preparation and Cooking Time: 5 minutes   **Serves 4**

Perfect for a picnic.

INGREDIENTS
4 hard-boiled eggs, chopped
2 cups cold cooked rice
1 cup chopped celery
½ cup chopped sweet pickles

DIRECTIONS
Combine eggs, rice, celery, pickles, pimiento, cheese and mayonnaise. Toss until well blended. Season to taste. Serve on crisp lettuce.

1 tablespoon chopped
    pimiento
1 cup shredded American
    cheddar cheese
¾ cup mayonnaise
Salt and freshly ground
    black pepper to taste
Crisp lettuce

CURRY RICE SALAD

Preparation and Cooking Time: 1 hour 5 minutes

Serves 4–6

Nuts, raisins and curry powder make this salad reminiscent of Indian food.

INGREDIENTS
½ cup raisins
1 cup warm water

3 cups cooked rice
1 tablespoon curry powder
1 cup hazel nuts
1 small can tiny peas,
    drained

1½ cups mayonnaise
Lemon juice to taste
Salt to taste

DIRECTIONS
Soak raisins for 1 hour in warm water.

Combine rice, drained raisins, hazel nuts and peas in a bowl.

Flavor mayonnaise with lemon juice. Mix salad with mayonnaise mixture and season with salt to taste.

ALMOND RICE SALAD

Preparation and Cooking Time: 1 hour 5 minutes

Serves 4–6

Chopped prunes and nuts add dash to this salad.

INGREDIENTS
1/2 cup prunes
Strong tea

2 small canned red
   peppers, diced
3 cups cooked rice
1/4 cup slivered almonds
1 tablespoon minced fresh
   parsley

2 tablespoons oil
2 tablespoons vinegar
Salt and freshly ground
   black pepper to taste

DIRECTIONS
Put prunes in a bowl and cover with strong tea. Soak at least 1 hour.

Remove pits from prunes and dice. In a large salad bowl, mix rice, peppers, prunes, almonds and parsley.

Mix together oil and vinegar; season with salt and black pepper. Pour over the salad, toss, and serve.

HOT ITALIAN RICE SALAD

Preparation and Cooking Time: 25 minutes*   **Serves 6**

Its flavors blend delicately in a hot rice salad. Hot vegetable salads tossed with olive oil and lemon or vinegar are Italian favorites.

INGREDIENTS
3 cups hot cooked rice
½ cup chopped celery
½ cup chopped green
    pepper
1 canned pimiento,
    chopped
2 tablespoons minced
    parsley
1 cup hot cooked peas
¼ cup sliced stuffed
    green olives
¼ cup sliced black olives
½ cup freshly grated
    Parmesan cheese

½ cup olive oil
Juice of 1 lemon
Freshly ground black
    pepper to taste

DIRECTIONS
Mix together gently hot well-drained rice, celery, green pepper, pimiento, parsley, peas, olives and cheese.

Toss gently with olive oil; then sprinkle with lemon juice and black pepper. Toss again. Add a little salt if necessary and serve at once.

*Does include rice cooking time.

CHICKEN, RICE AND AVOCADO SALAD

Preparation Time: 5 minutes   **Serves 6**

Avocado is both a pretty and delicious addition to salads.

INGREDIENTS
8 cups salad greens,
   washed, drained and torn
   apart (mixture of spinach,
   romaine, chicory, bibb,
   etc.)

6 hard-boiled eggs,
   quartered
1 avocado, peeled and cut
   in lengthwise slices
2 medium tomatoes, cut in
   wedges
½ teaspoon salt
1 cup sliced chicken pieces
1 cup cold cooked rice

To make dressing:
1 cup mayonnaise
¼ cup chili sauce
1 hard-boiled egg, finely
   chopped
8 pitted black olives, sliced
2 teaspoons minced chives
1 teaspoon lemon juice

DIRECTIONS
Clean salad greens and tear into bite-sized pieces. Put in large salad bowl. Set aside.

Arrange hard-boiled eggs, avocado, tomatoes, chicken and rice on top of salad greens. Sprinkle with salt.

Combine mayonnaise, chili sauce, chopped egg, olives, chives, and lemon juice. Mix well and chill. Serve with salad.

CHICKEN AND RICE STUFFED TOMATOES

Preparation Time: 10 minutes   **Serves 4**

Tomatoes stuffed with chicken, avocado and rice salad is a very good luncheon dish.

INGREDIENTS
1 large ripe avocado, diced
4 teaspoons lemon juice

1 cup diced cooked
   chicken
3/4 cup cooked rice
1/2 cup diced celery
1 teaspoon minced scallion
2 tablespoons mayonnaise
2 tablespoons sour cream
1 teaspoon salt

4 large ripe tomatoes
Crisp chilled lettuce

DIRECTIONS
Sprinkle avocado with lemon juice.

Combine remaining ingredients except tomatoes and lettuce. Mix well. Add avocado mixture and toss lightly.

Cut off tops of tomatoes and scoop out pulp. Discard pulp. Fill with chicken mixture. Serve on lettuce.

ATHENIAN SALAD

Preparation and Cooking Time: 30 minutes　　**Serves 4**

A pretty, colorful heated salad of ham, peaches and rice.

INGREDIENTS
1/4 cup butter
1 cup chopped ham
1/2 cup chopped green
　pepper

2 cups peach slices,
　drained
1 teaspoon lemon juice
1/2 cup olives
2 cups cooked rice

1/2 teaspoon salt
1/4 teaspoon freshly ground
　black pepper

Lettuce

DIRECTIONS
Sauté ham and peppers
in melted butter in a skillet for 5 minutes or until
peppers are limp.

Add peaches, lemon
juice, olives and cooked
rice. If you have time, allow this mixture to stand
at least 20 minutes to
blend flavors before
heating.

Sprinkle with salt and
pepper to taste; toss.

Serve on crisp, cold let-
tuce leaves.

SHRIMP AND RICE SALAD

Preparation and Cooking Time: 10 minutes   **Serves 4**

Hot rice salad is tossed with crisp, chilled lettuce just before serving.

INGREDIENTS
2 tablespoons butter
1 garlic clove, minced
4 green scallions, with top chopped

DIRECTIONS
Sauté garlic and scallions in butter until onions are limp and golden.

1 cup cooked shrimp, crab, lobster or fish
1 cup cooked rice
1 cup cooked string beans
Salt and freshly ground black pepper to taste

Add shrimp, rice, string beans, salt and black pepper. Mix; cover, and heat thoroughly, about 5 minutes. Add a little water if necessary.

1 cup chilled shredded lettuce

Just before serving, toss together with shredded lettuce.

CURRIED SHRIMP-RICE SALAD

Preparation and Cooking Time: 10 minutes   **Serves 4**

Crushed pineapple is an interesting addition.

INGREDIENTS	DIRECTIONS
1 cup chopped cooked shrimp 2 cups cold cooked rice ⅔ cup chopped celery 2 tablespoons chopped green pepper	Mix together shrimp, rice, celery and green pepper.
1 tablespoon minced onion ¾ teaspoon curry powder ¼ teaspoon dry mustard ½ teaspoon salt ⅛ teaspoon freshly ground black pepper ½ cup mayonnaise 1½ tablespoons lemon juice	Mix onion, curry powder, mustard, salt and pepper with mayonnaise. Stir in lemon juice. Toss shrimp mixture with mayonnaise mixture.
1 cup crushed pineapple, drained	Add pineapple and mix again.
Chilled lettuce leaves ¼ cup chopped salted peanuts	Serve on lettuce leaves with salted peanuts sprinkled over the top.

GINGER FLAVORED SHRIMP AND RICE SALAD

Preparation and Cooking Time: 5 minutes   **Serves 4**

Ginger and toasted sesame seeds add that little extra to a popular salad.

INGREDIENTS

3 scallions with tops, chopped fine
1 bunch chives, chopped fine
1 small onion, chopped fine
3 cups cold cooked rice

2 cups cooked, cleaned small shrimp
1 cup mayonnaise
Pinch of ginger
Salt to taste
Lemon juice to taste

Lettuce
Toasted sesame seeds

DIRECTIONS

Mix scallions, chives, onion and rice together.

Add shrimp and mayonnaise. Season to taste with ginger, salt and lemon juice; chill.

Heap on lettuce and garnish with toasted sesame seeds.

CRABMEAT AND RICE SALAD

Preparation and Cooking Time: 5 minutes   **Serves 4**

Curry powder adds a special flavor.

INGREDIENTS
1 medium green pepper, seeded and chopped
3 pimientos, chopped
2 cups cooked crabmeat, picked over and flaked

DIRECTIONS
Mix together green pepper, pimientos, crabmeat and rice.

1 cup mayonnaise
3/4 teaspoon curry powder
Salt to taste
Lemon juice to taste

Mix mayonnaise with curry powder, salt and lemon juice to taste. Mix into rice and crabmeat mixture; chill.

Lettuce
Minced chives

Serve on lettuce garnished with chives.

TOSSED FISH AND RICE SALAD

Preparation Time: 5 minutes   **Serves 4**

Lots of crunch and color.

INGREDIENTS
2 cups flaked cooked fish
1 cup cooked rice
1/2 cup chopped celery
1/2 cup cooked peas

DIRECTIONS
Combine fish, rice, celery, peas, pickle, onion, eggs, salt, mayonnaise and lemon juice; mix

235

2 tablespoons chopped
sweet pickle
2 tablespoons chopped
onion
2 hard-boiled eggs,
chopped
1 teaspoon salt
1/2 cup mayonnaise
2 tablespoons lemon juice

gently so fish will not be
broken into too small
pieces. Chill slightly.

Crisp chilled lettuce
4 cherry tomatoes
2 tablespoons capers,
drained

Serve on lettuce; garnish
with tomato and capers.

MOLDED CHICKEN, GRAPEFRUIT AND RICE SALAD

Preparation and Cooking Time: 10 minutes*   **Serves 6**

Cooling and refreshing.

INGREDIENTS
4 cups canned grapefruit

DIRECTIONS
Drain grapefruit sections,
reserving syrup. Set
aside.

2 envelopes unflavored
gelatin
1 3/4 cups cold water
2 chicken bouillon cubes

Sprinkle gelatin over cold
water in a saucepan. Add
bouillon cubes and stir
over moderate heat until

*Does not include chilling time.

gelatin and bouillon
cubes are dissolved.

1/2 teaspoon salt	Add reserved grapefruit syrup and salt. Chill until consistency is thick but not set.
1 cup diced, cooked chicken 3/4 cup cooked rice 2 teaspoon minced onion	Fold in drained grapefruit sections, chicken, rice, celery and onion. Turn into a 1½-quart mold and chill until firm.
Crisp chilled lettuce Pimiento strips	Unmold on salad greens and garnish with pimiento strips.

MOLDED CHICKEN AND RICE SALAD

Preparation Time: 10 minutes*   Serves 4

Crushed pineapple, diced celery, rice and pecans give this chicken salad an unusually elegant flair.

INGREDIENTS	DIRECTIONS
1 3-ounce package orange-pineapple gelatin 1/2 teaspoon salt 1¾ cups boiling chicken stock	Dissolve gelatin and salt in boiling chicken stock.
Dash of pepper Dash of paprika 2 tablespoons vinegar 1/4 cup mayonnaise	Add pepper, paprika, vinegar and mayonnaise; blend well. Chill until thick but not set.

*Does not include chilling time.

1½ cups diced, cooked chicken
¾ cup cooked rice
½ cup minced celery
1 tablespoon chopped pimiento
1 tablespoon minced fresh parsley
¼ cup canned crushed pineapple, drained
2 tablespoons coarsely chopped pecans
2 tablespoons sweet pickle relish

Fold in remaining ingredients. Pour into a 1½-quart mold. Chill until firm.

Crisp chilled lettuce
Cherry tomatoes
Sour cream or mayonnaise

Unmold on crisp lettuce leaves and surround with cherry tomatoes. Serve with sour cream or mayonnaise.

Desserts

BASIC DESSERT RICE

Preparation and Cooking Time: 20 minutes   **Serves 4**

This basic sweet rice can be used as a base for countless desserts. Just vary the flavorings and add nuts, fruit and dried and candied fruits and citron. Short-grain rices are best for desserts.

INGREDIENTS
3 cups milk, scalded
1/2 cup uncooked rice
Pinch of salt
5 tablespoons sugar

1 cup heavy cream
2 tablespoons butter

DIRECTIONS
Scald milk and add rice, salt and sugar. Cook until rice is tender and creamy.

When cooked, add cream and butter. Add more sugar if desired.

VARIATIONS
Rice flan or tart—Fill a dessert pie shell with dessert rice not quite to the top. Sprinkle with sugar. Cook at 350° F. for 25–30 minutes until golden. Serve hot or cold.

Chopped-up crystallized fruit soaked in kirsch or other liqueur is a happy addition.

Rice flan or tart with Fruit—Proceed as in the above recipe, but fill pie shell only ¾ full. Place raw apricots soaked in kirsch and sugar on top of rice. Sprinkle with sugar. Spread top of flan with apricot jam diluted with a little syrup and strained.

In the same way, flans can be made with various other fruits such as: bananas (cut in rounds or sliced lengthwise), cherries, pears (in quarters and half-cooked in syrup), peaches, apples, plums.

Rice with caramel—Fill a large Charlotte mold lined with caramelized sugar with dessert rice. Bake in oven in a pan of water for 25–30 minutes. Unmold. Serve hot or cold.

Rice with fruit—Layer dessert rice flavored with vanilla in a glass bowl, alternating with slices of fruit and a colorful fruit such as raspberries in syrup.

ALMOND RICE PUDDING

Preparation and Cooking Time: 40 minutes*   Serves 6–8

This dessert is served at Christmas by most Swedish families.

INGREDIENTS	DIRECTIONS
1¼ cups uncooked rice ⅔ cup sugar 1 teaspoon salt 6 cups milk	Combine rice, sugar, salt and milk in a large saucepan. Bring to a boil; reduce heat and simmer, uncovered, for 20 minutes, stirring frequently. Remove from heat. Cool slightly.
¼ cup cream sherry 1 tablespoon vanilla 1 cup toasted, slivered almonds	Stir in sherry, vanilla and almonds.
2 cups heavy cream	Whip cream until soft peaks form. Fold into rice mixture. Cover and chill overnight. Serve with lingonberry preserves.

*Does not include chilling time.

CREAMY RICE PUDDING

Preparation and Cooking Time: 1 hour   Serves 4

An easy, one-pot pudding.

INGREDIENTS
2½ cups milk
½ cup uncooked rice
½ teaspoon salt
¼ cup sugar
⅛ teaspoon nutmeg
⅛ teaspoon cinnamon
½ cup raisins

Heavy cream

DIRECTIONS
Scald milk in top of a double boiler. Add other ingredients slowly, stirring constantly. Cook covered over hot water until rice has absorbed milk, about 1 hour. Stir frequently.

Serve warm with cream.

DANISH ALMOND-RICE PUDDING

Preparation and Cooking Time: 1 hour*   Serves 4–6

A traditional pudding filled with almonds and flavored with sherry.

INGREDIENTS
½ cup uncooked rice
1 quart milk
1 vanilla bean or
  1 teaspoon vanilla
½ teaspoon salt

DIRECTIONS
Bring milk to a boil; add rice, stirring constantly, and vanilla and salt. Cook over medium heat for 5 minutes, stirring constantly. Cover and cook over very low heat

*Does not include chilling time.

for 45 minutes, stirring occasionally. Discard vanilla.

½ cup ground blanched almonds
¼ cup sugar

Mix in almonds and sugar and let stand until cold.

2 cups heavy cream
3 tablespoons sweet sherry or to taste

Whip cream and fold into rice mixture with sherry. Chill and serve with warmed cherry or raspberry jam if desired.

DUTCH APPLE RICE

Preparation and Cooking Time: 20 minutes* Serves 4–6

A yummy top-of-the stove favorite.

INGREDIENTS
2 cups cooked rice
½ cup milk
⅓ cup raisins
1 egg, beaten
1/3 cup sugar
½ teaspoon salt
¼ teaspoon cinnamon
1 tablespoon butter

DIRECTIONS
Combine rice, milk, raisins, egg, sugar, salt, cinnamon and butter in a large saucepan. Simmer on top of stove, stirring occasionally, until blended.

2 cups cooked, peeled apple slices

Stir in apple slices. Pour into serving dishes and chill.

*Does not include chilling time.

Dash of nutmeg | Sprinkle with nutmeg before serving.

GERMAN RICE PUDDING

Preparation and Cooking Time: 45 minutes   **Serves 6**

A very creamy pudding cooked on top of the range.

INGREDIENTS
1/2 cup uncooked rice
2 cups boiling water

DIRECTIONS
Put rice and water into a saucepan. Bring to a boil; reduce heat and cook, stirring occasionally, until all water is absorbed.

3 cups milk
1/2 cup sugar
1/4 teaspoon salt
1 teaspoon vanilla

Stir in milk and simmer for 20 minutes, stirring occasionally. Add sugar and salt; cook for 20 more minutes until mixture is creamy. Stir in vanilla.

Cinnamon
Applesauce

Serve warm, sprinkled with cinnamon. Top with a spoonful of applesauce.

ORANGE RICE AU GRAND MARNIER

Preparation and Cooking Time: 30 minutes*   **Serves 6**

Flavoring orange rice pudding with Grand Marnier makes it a dish fit for a king.

INGREDIENTS
¾ cup uncooked rice
3 cups milk
Pinch of salt

1½ teaspoons grated
    orange rind
½ cup orange juice
¾ cup heavy cream,
    whipped

2 cups orange sections
1/3 cup Grand Marnier

DIRECTIONS
Cook rice in milk with a pinch of salt in a covered saucepan over low heat until tender, about 20 minutes. Cool slightly.

Mix rice with orange rind, orange juice and whipped cream.

Layer rice mixture with orange sections; top with Grand Marnier. Chill if desired.

*Does not include cooling time.

PINEAPPLE RICE PUDDING

Preparation and Cooking Time: 30 minutes*   **Serves 6**

Whipped cream and pineapple is folded into chilled creamy rice before serving.

INGREDIENTS	DIRECTIONS
6 tablespoons uncooked rice 2 cups milk 1/4 cup sugar Pinch of salt	Combine rice, milk, sugar and salt in top of a double boiler; cook over boiling water, stirring constantly, until rice is tender, about 20 minutes. Remove from heat.
1/2 teaspoon vanilla 1/4 teaspoon nutmeg 1/4 cup milk	Stir in vanilla, nutmeg and milk. Refrigerate until well chilled.
1/2 cup heavy cream, whipped 1/2 cup crushed pineapple, drained	Fold in whipped cream and pineapple before serving.

*Does not include chilling time.

POLISH RICE WITH PLUMS

Preparation and Cooking Time: 10 minutes*   **Serves 4**

This recipe is a good way to use up leftovers.

INGREDIENTS	DIRECTIONS
2 cups cooked rice 2 cups pitted plums	Arrange rice and plums in layers. Put the rice first, then fruit.
1 tablespoon sugar 1/2 teaspoon cinnamon	Sprinkle with cinnamon and sugar. Continue until all ingredients are used up. Refrigerate for 2 hours.
1 cup sour cream 3 tablespoons sugar	Beat sour cream with sugar. Serve over top of chilled rice.

VARIATION
Use sliced peaches or other fruit instead of plums.

*Does not include chilling time.

RICE ROMANOFF

Preparation and Cooking Time: 10 minutes   Serves 4–6

Flavored with liqueur and filled with toasted almonds, this dessert is a great ending for any important dinner.

INGREDIENTS
DIRECTIONS

3 cups heavy cream
3 tablespoons kirsch, Grand Marnier or cognac
3 tablespoons sugar

Whip cream until stiff and flavor with liquor and sugar.

1/2 cup blanched, slivered almonds
3 cups cooked rice

Stir in almonds. Mix cream mixture thoroughly with rice. Place ⅓ of rice cream in a large glass serving bowl.

20 macaroons, soaked in kirsch, Grand Marnier or cognac

Arrange macaroons on top. Add another third of rice cream, then remaining macaroons. Finish with rice cream. Chill. Serve with raspberry sauce.

STRAWBERRY RICE PARFAIT

Preparation and Cooking Time: 30 minutes*   **Serves 4**

Strawberries and whipped cream make this one of the prettiest and tastiest desserts you can serve.

INGREDIENTS
1 cup uncooked rice
2½ tablespoons sugar
2 cups cold water

DIRECTIONS
Put rice, sugar and cold water in a saucepan; bring to a fast boil. Stir rice and lower heat; cover ond simmer for 15 minutes or until rice is tender. Do not lift cover during this time. Chill rice.

½ pint heavy cream
2 tablespoons sugar
½ teaspoon almond extract

Just before serving, whip heavy cream; fold in sugar and almond flavoring. Fold into chilled rice.

1 package frozen strawberries, thawed

Fill parfait glasses with alternate layers of rice mixture and strawberries, ending with whipped cream and a strawberry on top.

*Does not include chilling time.

SWEDISH RICE PORRIDGE

Preparation and Cooking Time: 1 hour 15 minutes

Serves 6–8

This dish is as much a part of the Christmas celebration in Sweden as the Christmas tree or Santa Claus.

INGREDIENTS
2 cups uncooked rice, rinsed in hot water
2 cups water

2 tablespoons butter
2 quarts milk
2 teaspoons salt
2 tablespoons sugar
Large 3-inch piece of cinnamon bark

1 teaspoon butter
Sugar
Ground cinnamon
Cold milk

DIRECTIONS
Bring water to a boil; add rice and cook until water is absorbed.

Melt butter in a large pot; add milk and bring to a boil. Add salt, sugar, cinnamon bark and rice. Cook over lowered heat for 1 hour or until rice is tender. Add more milk if necessary.

Pour porridge into a large bowl. Bury butter in center. Sprinkle top generously with sugar and cinnamon. Serve with cold milk.

VARIATION
Bury an almond in the center of the porridge. Whoever gets the almond will marry during the ensuing year.

AUNT ROSIE'S RICE PUDDING

Preparation and Baking Time: 1 hour 15 minutes **Serves 6**

A superb basic rice pudding filled with plump raisins which my Aunt Rosie, Mrs. Louis Ronzitti, makes.

INGREDIENTS
3 cups milk

DIRECTIONS
Scald or heat milk in a saucepan until almost boiling; allow hot milk to cool slightly.

3 large eggs, beaten
1/2 cup sugar
1/2 teaspoon salt

Mix together eggs, sugar and salt in a 1½-quart baking dish. Add hot milk slowly, stirring constantly.

1 cup cooked rice
1 teaspoon vanilla
1/2 cup raisins

Stir in cooked rice, vanilla and raisins. Place baking dish in a pan containing an inch of hot water in oven. Bake at 350° F. for 1 hour or until set. Stir once after pudding has been in oven 15 minutes.

BAKED APPLE-DATE RICE PUDDING

Preparation and Cooking Time: **Serves 6**

Apples and dates complement each other in this easy dessert.

INGREDIENTS
2 medium apples, cored, peeled and chopped fine
2 cups cooked rice
1/2 cup milk
2 eggs, beaten
3/4 cup sugar
2 tablespoons melted butter
1/2 cup chopped pitted dates
1 teaspoon vanilla

DIRECTIONS
Combine apples, rice, milk, eggs, sugar, butter, dates and vanilla; stir together until blended. Pour into a greased casserole; set in a pan of hot water. Bake at 350° F. for 45 minutes. Chill.

1 cup cream, whipped
Toasted coconut

Top each serving with whipped cream and toasted coconut.

*Does not include chilling time.

APRICOT PUDDING

Preparation and Cooking Time: 30 minutes   **Serves 4**

Apricot jam makes this pudding both pretty and delicious.

INGREDIENTS
1 cup cooked rice
1/4 cup sugar
Pinch of salt
2 eggs, beaten

DIRECTIONS
Combine rice with sugar and salt. Fold eggs which have been beaten until very thick and lemon colored into rice mixture.

2/3 cup milk
2/3 cup light cream
1 tablespoon grated lemon rind
3 tablespoons apricot jam
1/3 cup chopped almonds or pecans

Mix with milk, cream, lemon rind and 1 tablespoon apricot jam. Pour into buttered baking dish. Spread with rest of apricot jam and sprinkle with almonds. Bake in a 350° F. oven for 20 minutes or until pudding is firm and golden.

Sour cream

Serve warm with sour cream.

BRANDIED RICE PUDDING

Preparation and Cooking Time: I hour   **Serves 8**

Real brandy turns a good rice pudding into something special.

INGREDIENTS
5 cups cooked rice
2 eggs, beaten
I cup sugar
2 cups raisins
I teaspoon cinnamon
2 tablespoons butter, melted

DIRECTIONS
Mix together rice, eggs, sugar, raisins, cinnamon and butter. Pour into buttered casserole. Bake in preheated 300° F. oven for 45 minutes.

½ cup brandy
Powdered sugar
I cup light cream

Turn out on a warmed dish; pour brandy over the top. Sprinkle with powdered sugar and serve with cream separately.

RICE PUDDING WITH CANDIED FRUIT

Preparation and Cooking Time: I hour   **Serves 6**

A spectacular dessert garnished with whipped cream and raspberry jam or both.

INGREDIENTS
3 cups milk
3 cups cooked rice

DIRECTIONS
Scald milk in a saucepan. Add rice and cook cov-

256

	ered for 15 minutes. Remove from heat.
¾ cup sugar 2 tablespoons butter 4 eggs, beaten	Add sugar, butter, eggs and blend well.
2 teaspoons vanilla ¾ cup candied fruit soaked in 2½ tablespoons rum Pinch of salt	Add vanilla, candied fruit soaked in rum and a pinch of salt.
¼ cup sugar 2 tablespoons sugar	Melt remaining sugar with water in a charlotte mold or other straight-sided baking dish. When sugar is light brown, tilt mold so syrup will cover the bottom and sides. Fill with rice mixture and place in a pan of hot water. Bake for 30 minutes at 350° F. Cool to lukewarm.
Whipped cream or melted raspberry jam	Unmold and garnish with whipped cream or melted raspberry jam.

ORANGE RICE CUSTARD

Preparation and Cooking Time: 50 minutes   **Serves 6**

An orange-flavored rice custard which can be served with chicken or duck or topped with honey for dessert.

INGREDIENTS
1 cup uncooked rice
2½ cups scalded milk
Pinch of salt

DIRECTIONS
Cook rice in milk with a pinch of salt in a covered saucepan over low heat until tender, about 20 minutes.

3 eggs, beaten
1 tablespoon butter
Juice of 1 orange
2 tablespoons grated orange rind
1 tablespoon sesame seeds

Mix rice with eggs, butter, orange juice, rind and sesame seeds. Bake for 25 minutes until custard is set in a 300° F. oven.

BAKED PEACH AND RICE CUSTARD

Preparation and Cooking Time: 1 hour   **Serves 4**

Peaches and rice are alternated in this marvelously tasty custard dessert.

INGREDIENTS
2½ cups milk
2 eggs, beaten
¼ cup sugar
½ teaspoon salt

DIRECTIONS
Combine milk, eggs, sugar and salt in top of a double boiler; cook over boiling water, stirring

constantly, 20 minutes or until thickened. Remove from heat.

2 cups cooked rice 1/2 teaspoon almond extract	Stir in rice and almond extract.
2 cups canned peaches, drained	In buttered casserole, alternate layers of peaches and rice, beginning with rice and ending with colorful peaches.
2 tablespoons brown sugar	Top with brown sugar. Bake for 30 minutes at 350° F. or until custard is set. Serve warm or cold with cream.

RICE MELBA

Preparation and Cooking Time: 25 minutes*   **Serves 6**

As beautiful and tasty as the original made with ice cream.

INGREDIENTS	DIRECTIONS
2/3 cup uncooked rice 2 cups milk	Combine rice and milk in a saucepan. Bring to a boil; cover and simmer gently for 16 minutes. Remove rice from heat.
1/3 cup sugar 1/4 teaspoon salt Pinch of nutmeg	Stir in sugar, salt, nutmeg and cinnamon. Cool slightly. Then chill rice

*Does not include chilling time.

Pinch of cinnamon	quickly in freezer but do not let it freeze.
1 cup heavy cream 6 canned peach halves, drained	Whip cream. Fold chilled rice into cream. Spoon into dessert dishes. Put peach half on top, cut side down.
1/2 cup red currant or raspberry jelly	Heat jelly and pour a little over each peach.

RICE A L'IMPERATRICE

Preparation and Cooking Time: 1 hour*   Serves 6

Candied fruit, kirsch, walnuts and whipped cream combine to make this creamy dessert both extraordinarily good and impressively decorative for your most important dinners.

INGREDIENTS	DIRECTIONS
3/4 cup mixed candied fruits, finely chopped 1/3 cup kirsch	Marinate fruits in kirsch. Set aside.
1/2 cup walnuts, chopped 1/4 cup kirsch	Marinate nuts in kirsch. Set aside.
1/2 cup uncooked rice 1 3/4 cups milk	Cook rice in milk until tender, about 20 minutes, over low heat. Cover saucepan when cooking.
4 egg yolks, beaten 1/2 cup sugar	Meanwhile, combine egg yolks with sugar, milk

*Does not include chilling time.

¾ cup milk	and vanilla in top of a
½ teaspoon vanilla extract	double boiler. Cook over
	boiling water, stirring
	constantly, until thick-
	ened.

| 1 envelope unflavored gelatin | Soften gelatin in cold water; stir into milk-egg mixture. Add rice and blend well. Chill until mixture begins to set. |
| 2 tablespoons cold water | |

| 1 cup heavy cream, whipped | Fold in ½ cup marinated fruit and whipping cream. Spoon rice mixture into an 8-inch ring mold. Chill at least 4 hours; unmold. |

| ⅔ cup currant jelly | Mix marinated nuts into jelly; sprinkle on top and around mold. Decorate with remaining fruit. |

RICE AND RICOTTA CHEESE BAKE

Preparation and Cooking Time: 40 minutes   **Serves 4**

Warmed jam tops this easy-to-prepare baked rice dessert made with ricotta cheese.

INGREDIENTS	DIRECTIONS
2 egg yolks, beaten	Beat egg yolks with sugar;
3 tablespoons sugar	combine with cheese un-
1¼ cups ricotta cheese	til well blended.

261

2 cups cooked rice	Add to rice and mix well.
2 egg whites, beaten stiff **½ cup bread crumbs**	Fold in egg whites; pour into a buttered tube pan which has been sprinkled with bread crumbs. Bake in a preheated 400° F. oven for 30 minutes.
1 cup raspberry, peach or currant jam, warmed	Remove from pan. Serve hot or cold with warmed jam poured over the top.

APRICOT RICE SOUFFLÉ

Preparation and Cooking Time: 1 hour 30 minutes **Serves 4**

Soufflés have an undeserved reputation for being difficult to make. This delicious dessert will prove otherwise.

INGREDIENTS

DIRECTIONS

¼ cup butter **¼ cup flour** **1 cup milk** **½ teaspoon salt**	In a large saucepan, stir flour into melted butter to make a roux. Blend in milk and salt. Cook, stirring constantly, until thickened. Remove from heat. Cool slightly.
4 egg yolks, slightly beaten **1 cup cooked rice**	Combine white sauce with beaten egg yolks and rice.
1 cup apricot pulp **⅓ cup sugar** **1 tablespoon apricot brandy or to taste**	Add apricot pulp, sugar and apricot brandy to rice mixture; mix thoroughly.

4 egg whites, beaten until stiff but not dry	Fold in beaten egg whites. Pour into an ungreased 2-quart casserole. Bake for 1 hour in a preheated 325° F. oven. Serve immediately.

POACHED PEARS WITH LEMON RICE CREAM SAUCE

Preparation and Cooking Time: 5 minutes* **Serves 4**

An outstanding sauce for cooked fruit.

INGREDIENTS
1 cup heavy cream, whipped
2 tablespoons sugar
1 tablespoon lemon juice
1/2 teaspoon grated lemon rind
1/4 teaspoon vanilla
Dash of nutmeg
1 cup cold cooked rice

DIRECTIONS
Whip cream. Add sugar, lemon juice and rind, vanilla and nutmeg. Fold into cold rice and chill.

4 chilled whole poached pears

Top individual-poached pears with cream sauce before serving.

*Does not include chilling time.

RICE CAKE WITH CARAMEL SAUCE

Preparation and Baking Time: 1 hour 45 minutes

Serves 6–8

A rich rice custard topped with caramel.

INGREDIENTS
2 cups sugar
1/4 cup water

DIRECTIONS
Cook sugar in water in a heavy saucepan until you reach a candy consistency and the color becomes light brown. Be careful not to let sugar burn.

When done, pour caramel into a 2½-quart round baking dish, rotating the dish so that the sides and bottom are evenly coated with caramel. Set aside.

1/2 cup uncooked rice
1 teaspoon salt
3 cups water

Put rice and salt in water in a large saucepan; bring to a boil. Cover and simmer over moderate heat until tender, about 20 minutes.

3 tablespoons butter

Remove from heat and stir in butter.

6 eggs, beaten
4 cups light cream, scalded
1 cup sugar

Beat eggs in a large mixing bowl. Add cream, sugar, vanilla and rind. Add rice into egg-cream

1 tablespoon vanilla
Rind of 1 orange

mixture. Pour mixture into caramelized baking dish. Set into shallow baking pan half filled with hot water and bake in a preheated 300° F. oven for 1 hour or until done. When ready, a knife inserted in the center should come out clean. Cool. Unmold onto a platter with a rim to catch the surplus caramel sauce.

RICE CAKE

Preparation and Baking Time: 2 hours*

Makes 1 12-inch cake

Filled with candied citron and almonds.

INGREDIENTS
6½ cups milk
1½ cups rice
Pinch of salt
½ cup sugar

DIRECTIONS
Bring milk to a boil in a saucepan; stir in rice, salt and sugar. Simmer gently until rice is almost tender. When rice is ready, remove from heat and allow to cool.

4 egg yolks
½ cup sugar

Beat egg yolks with remaining sugar. Stir in

*Does not include cooling time.

Grated rind of 1 lemon or orange
½ cup diced candied citron
1 teaspoon vanilla
½ cup toasted chopped almonds

rice mixture, grated rind, diced candied peel vanilla, and almonds.

4 egg whites, at room temperature

Beat egg whites until stiff and fold into mixture.

Fine dry bread crumbs

Butter well a 12-inch cake pan; coat with bread crumbs. Pour rice mixture into pan. Bake at 325° F. for 1½ hours. The cake should be firm and light with a golden brown top. Cool.

¼ cup Maraschino

Prick when cool with a toothpick; sprinkle with Maraschino.

Powdered sugar

Allow to lay overnight. Dust with powdered sugar before serving.

PASTIERA NAPOLETANA

Neapolitan Cheese Pie

Preparation and Baking Time: 1 hour 30 minutes
Makes 1 10-inch pie

My sister-in-law Mrs. Michael (Gerri) Torre gave me this recipe for this delicately flavored cheese pie. The rice adds a nutty texture.

INGREDIENTS
To make filling:
2½ cups milk
⅔ cup uncooked rice
Pinch of salt

DIRECTIONS
Scald milk in a saucepan; stir in rice and salt. Cook until rice is tender and has absorbed milk. Cool.

1 pound ricotta
1½ cups sugar

Put ricotta and sugar in a mixing bowl; beat until smooth.

4 eggs

Add eggs one at a time, beating well after each addition.

½ cup raisins or citron
1 teaspoon vanilla
Grated rind of 1 orange

Add raisins, orange rind and vanilla; blend well. Fold in cooked rice. Pour mixture into prepared pie pan and top with lattice strips. Flute edges. Bake in a preheated 425° F.

267

oven for 15 minutes; lower heat to 350° F. and continue baking for another 45 minutes or until firm in the center.

PASTIERA DI GRANO

Neapolitan Easter Grain Pie

Preparation and Baking Time: 1 hour 30 minutes
                    Makes 1 12-inch round cake

The original uses whole wheat softened for 3 days and cooked in milk. This version using rice is just as delicious. Chocolate is the secret.

INGREDIENTS
To make pie crust
    (pasta frolla):
2 cups flour
1/2 cup sugar
Pinch of salt
1/4 cup butter
3 egg yolks
1 tablespoon grated lemon
    or orange rind
1 tablespoon milk

DIRECTIONS
Sift together flour, salt and sugar into a bowl; cut in butter with a pastry blender or with finger tips. Stir in egg yolks and rind.
Work with hands until dough is manageable, adding a little milk, if necessary, to hold together. Put on lightly floured board and knead quickly until smooth. Form into a ball and chill

for 30 minutes. *Make filling while dough is chilling.*

When ready, divide ball into two parts, one larger than the other. Roll out on floured board and line pie plate, leaving a ½-inch overhang. Fill with filling and top with ¾ inch strips for a lattice top.

Make pasta frolla and chill it.

To make filling:

2 squares baking chocolate	Preheat oven to 350° F. Melt chocolate in a small double boiler; cool.
1 pound ricotta 1½ cups sugar 3 eggs	Put ricotta, sugar and eggs in a large mixing bowl and beat until smooth.
Grated rind of 1 orange 1 tablespoon candied citron 1 teaspoon vanilla	Add orange rind, citron, vanilla and chocolate; stir until well blended.
1½ cups cooked rice	Lastly fold in the cooked rice.

Divide chilled dough into two parts, one larger than the other. Roll out on floured board and line bottom of a 12-inch cake or spring-form pan. Spread it out, pushing

269

with your fingers, up the sides about 1½ inches. Pour in ricotta mixture. Top with ¾ inch strips for a lattice top.

1 egg white, beaten

Brush with a bit of beaten egg white. Bake in a 350° F. oven for 1 hour or until pie is nicely browned. Cool before serving.

RICE TARTS

Preparation and Baking Time: 1 hour 30 minutes **Makes 12**

Flaky tarts filled with creamy rice.

INGREDIENTS
To make dough:
1/4 cup sugar
1 teaspoon grated lemon rind
2 cups flour, sifted
8 tablespoons butter

DIRECTIONS
Mix sugar, lemon rind and flour together; blend in butter.

2 egg yolks, beaten
4 tablespoons cold water

Mix egg yolks blended with water into sugar mixture. Form into a smooth ball. Roll out thinly on floured board; line buttered tart pans. Chill.

To make filling:
1/3 cup uncooked rice

Cook rice, milk, cream,

270

1⅔ cups milk
⅓ cup cream
Pinch of salt
½ cup sugar

salt and sugar in top of a
double boiler until rice is
tender; allow to cool.

2 egg yolks, beaten
½ teaspoon vanilla
½ teaspoon grated lemon
 rind
3 tablespoons butter,
 melted
2 egg whites, beaten stiff

Add egg yolks, vanilla,
lemon rind and butter;
fold in egg whites. Fill
chilled tarts; bake for 20
minutes at 400° F. Serve
with whipped cream.

KOLWADJIK

Preparation and Cooking Time: 45 minutes*
Makes one 13- by 9-inch cake

Cape Malays contributed this rice cake to the South African dessert repertoire.

INGREDIENTS
1¼ cups regular,
 long-grain rice
Water

DIRECTIONS
Boil rice until very soft.
Drain.

½ cup sugar
1 teaspoon cinnamon
¼ teaspoon cardamon
¼ cup butter
1 to 2 cups shredded
 coconut

Combine rice with sugar,
cinnamon, cardamon, but-
ter and coconut. Press
into a baking pan (13-
by-9-by-2 inches) and
cool. Cut into diamonds
and serve like cake.

*Does not include cooling time.

DESSERT RICE PANCAKES

Preparation and Cooking Time: 20 minutes **Serves 4**

Sweetened rice filled with plump raisins is browned lightly in butter.

INGREDIENTS	DIRECTIONS
1 cup cooked rice 2 tablespoons raisins 1/3 cup milk	Simmer rice, raisins and milk in a covered saucepan over low heat until milk is absorbed.
1 egg 2 tablespoons sugar	Remove from heat and mix in egg and sugar. Add a little milk if too dry.
2 tablespoons butter	Heat butter on a griddle. Drop mixture by tablespoonfuls and spread into 3-inch rounds. Brown lightly on both sides. Keep warm while browning the rest.
Warm honey or preserves	Serve with warm honey or preserves.

APRICOT FILLED RICE CREPES

Preparation and Cooking Time: 30 minutes

Makes 10 crepes

Canned pie filling makes this an easy dessert.

INGREDIENTS	DIRECTIONS
To make crepes:	Sift flour, salt and sugar together into a bowl.
½ cup flour	
¼ teaspoon salt	
1 tablespoon sugar	
2 eggs, beaten	Mix together eggs, milk, water and butter. Add slowly to dry ingredients, beating until smooth.
½ cup milk	
1 tablespoon cold water	
1 tablespoon melted butter or margarine	
½ cup cooked rice	Mix in rice. Let stand at room temperature 10 minutes.
	To make crepes, brush bottom and sides of a 6-inch crepe pan or skillet with cooking oil and set over moderate heat. Stir batter; then add 2 tablespoons to skillet, tipping it back and forth so batter just coats bottom. Brown lightly on 1 side; turn and brown the other side.

Keep warm in a 250° F. oven until all are done. Cook remaining crepes the same way.

To make filling:
1 can apricot pie filling
Powdered sugar

Heat pie filling. To serve, spread with pie filling, roll and sprinkle with powdered sugar.

DESSERT RICE BALLS

Preparation and Cooking Time: 30 minutes*   Serves 4

Sweetened rice balls are topped with sour cream.

INGREDIENTS	DIRECTIONS
1 cup rice 2 cups milk 4 tablespoons sugar	Cook rice in sweetened milk in a covered saucepan on low heat until tender, about 20 minutes. Cool.
1 teaspoon grated lemon rind 1 teaspoon lemon juice Pinch of salt 1 tablespoon butter 1/2 teaspoon vanilla	Mix with lemon rind, lemon juice, salt, butter and vanilla. Form balls the size of walnuts. Chill.
4 tablespoons sour cream 1 tablespoon cinnamon sugar	Serve topped with sour cream and sprinkled with cinnamon sugar.

*Does not include chilling time.

STRAWBERRY-RICE ICE CREAM

Preparation and Cooking Time: 15 minutes*   **Serves 4**

Rice adds a nutlike texture to ice cream.

INGREDIENTS
3/4 cup hot cooked rice
1 cup milk
1/2 cup cream

2 eggs, beaten

1 15-ounce can condensed
   milk
2 tablespoons sugar
Pinch of salt

2 cups milk

1 large package frozen
   strawberries in syrup,
   thawed
2 tablespoons lemon juice
   or juice from 1 small
   lemon

DIRECTIONS
Mash rice while hot with
a fork. Place in a sauce-
pan with milk and cream.

Add beaten eggs to hot
rice mixture. Cook about
1 minute, stirring con-
stantly.

Add condensed milk,
sugar and salt; stir well.

Stir in milk. To tray-
freeze, freeze until
mushy.

When mushy turn into
bowl, beat thoroughly;
stir in strawberries and
lemon juice. Freeze until
firm in trays.

VARIATIONS
Substitute your favorite
fruit such as crushed

*Does not include freezing time.

pineapple or peaches for strawberries.

ALMONDETTES

Preparation and Baking Time: 45 minutes   **Makes 3 dozen**

Crisp and fancy.

INGREDIENTS
3 eggs
1 cup sugar

1 cup sifted rice flour
1/4 teaspoon salt
1/2 teaspoon almond extract
1/2 up blanched, slivered almonds

DIRECTIONS
Beat eggs and sugar together until very thick and light.

Fold in rice flour, salt, almond extract and nuts. Drop by teaspoonfuls onto lightly greased baking sheet. Bake at 350° F. for about 15 minutes.

Breads
and
Stuffings

CALAS

Fried Cakes

Preparation and Cooking Time: 1 hour*   Serves 6

These delicious little fried cakes sprinkled with sugar and cinnamon are favorites in New Orleans with morning coffee.

INGREDIENTS
½ package dry yeast
½ cup warm water

DIRECTIONS
Dissolve yeast in warm water.

1½ cups cooked rice
mashed and cooled to
lukewarm

Stir in lukewarm rice; mix well. Cover and let rise in a warm place overnight.

3 eggs, beaten
1¼ cups flour, sifted
¼ cup sugar
½ teaspoon salt
¼ teaspoon nutmeg

Add eggs, flour, sugar, salt and nutmeg; beat until smooth. Let stand in a warm place 30 minutes.

Oil for frying
Powdered sugar or sugar
and cinnamon

Heat oil to 375° F. Drop mixture by spoonfuls into hot oil and fry until golden brown, about 3 minutes. Drain on absorbent paper. Serve hot, sprinkled with powdered sugar or sugar mixed with cinnamon.

VARIATIONS
These cakes are also excellent served with fruit or maple syrup.

RICE MUFFINS

Preparation and Baking Time: 45 minutes   Makes 12

Muffins made without yeast are typical of native American cookery. Moist and chewy, rice muffins are quick and easy to make.

INGREDIENTS
1½ cups flour
2 teaspoons baking powder
½ teaspoon salt
2 tablespoons sugar

DIRECTIONS
Preheat oven to 425° F. Sift flour, baking powder, salt and sugar together in a large mixing bowl.

3 tablespoons shortening

Cut in shortening with a pastry blender until mixture is crumbly.

1 cup cold cooked rice
1 cup milk
1 egg, beaten

Add rice, milk and egg; mix until dry ingredients are moistened. Batter will be lumpy and rough.

Bake for 25 minutes or until golden brown. Serve hot.

SOUTHERN RICE POPOVERS

Preparation and Baking Time: 50 minutes   Serves 4–6

Light and tasty.

INGREDIENTS
½ cup cold cooked rice
1 cup sifted flour
1 teaspoon baking powder
1 teaspoon grated orange rind
½ teaspoon salt
3 teaspoons sugar

1 egg yolk
2 teaspoons melted butter

1 egg white, beaten

DIRECTIONS
Preheat oven to 425° F. and heat buttered popover molds. Combine rice with flour, baking powder, orange rind, salt and sugar. Blend well.

Add egg yolk and melted butter; mix again.

Fold in beaten egg white. Fill heated buttered molds half full with batter. Bake for 25 minutes until tops are firm and golden brown. Reduce heat to 350° F. and bake for 10 minutes more. Prick popovers with tines of a fork to allow steam to escape. Turn off heat, place on a baking sheet and allow to remain in the oven 10 minutes more.

281

PHILPY

Preparation and Baking Time: 45 minutes

Makes 1 9-inch round loaf

A lovely hot bread from the South. Serve with chicken or pork.

INGREDIENTS
1/3 cup uncooked rice
1 cup milk

DIRECTIONS
Put rice and milk into a pot; cover and cook over low heat for 20 minutes. When done, milk will be absorbed and rice soft.

1/2 cup flour
2 egg yolks
1 teaspoon salt
2 tablespoons sugar
1/3 cup milk

Stir in flour, egg yolks, salt, sugar and milk.

1/3 cup sour cream
2 egg whites, beaten until stiff

Add sour cream and fold in stiffly beaten egg whites. Put batter in a well-greased 9-inch pie plate and bake at 375° F. for 20 minutes or until golden. Serve hot with butter and honey.

RICE DUMPLINGS

Preparation and Cooking Time: 20 minutes   **Serves 4–6**

Try these chewy dumplings in your favorite stew.
Add fresh mint or fresh dill if you have it.

INGREDIENTS
1¼ cups cooked rice
2/3 cup flour
2 teaspoons baking powder
¾ teaspoon salt
1 egg, beaten
¼ cup milk
1 tablespoon melted butter
Chopped dill or mint

DIRECTIONS
Mix all ingredients together to make a stiff but light dough. Flavor with mint or dill if you have it. Form into balls; roll in flour and drop into a simmering stew. Cover and cook for 15 minutes without lifting the lid.

RICE WAFFLES

Preparation and Cooking Time: 15 minutes   **Serves 4–6**

Light and chewy, these waffles are topped with a honey and cinnamon sauce.

INGREDIENTS
To make waffles:
1¾ cups flour
4 teaspoons baking powder
¼ teaspoon salt
2/3 cup cold cooked rice

DIRECTIONS
Sift flour, baking powder and salt together; mix with rice.

1⅓ cups milk
1 egg yolk, beaten
1 tablespoon melted butter

Combine milk, egg yolks and butter, add to dry ingredients and mix well.

283

2 **egg whites, beaten stiff**

Fold in egg whites. Cook on a lightly greased hot waffle iron; serve with butter and honey syrup sauce.

To make sauce:
1 cup honey
½ cup maple syrup
1 teaspoon powdered cinnamon

Combine honey, maple syrup and cinnamon; heat. Serve over hot waffles.

SOUTHERN RICE BUTTERMILK WAFFLES

Preparation and Cooking Time: 20 minutes   **Serves 4**

Tender delicate waffles.

INGREDIENTS
3 eggs, separated
2 cups buttermilk
6 tablespoons melted shortening

DIRECTIONS
Beat egg yolks until thick and lemon colored. Add buttermilk and shortening.

2 cups sifted flour
½ teaspoon salt
1 tablespoon baking powder
1 teaspoon sugar
½ teaspoon baking soda

Sift together flour, salt, baking powder, sugar and baking soda. Add to egg-buttermilk mixture. Stir until smooth.

1 cup cooked rice

Stir in rice.

Beat egg whites until stiff and fold into rice mixture. Bake on a hot waffle iron. Serve with lots of butter and your favorite fruit preserves.

RICE PANCAKES

Preparation and Cooking Time: 20 minutes   Serves 4–6

Rice adds an almost nutlike quality to pancakes.

INGREDIENTS	DIRECTIONS
2 cups flour, sifted 2 teaspoons baking powder 1 teaspoon salt 2 tablespoons sugar	Sift together dry ingredients in a large mixing bowl.
4 egg yolks, beaten 5 tablespoons shortening 2 cups milk	Combine egg yolks, shortening and milk. Stir into dry ingredients; mix well.
1½ cups cold cooked rice	Add rice to batter; blend well.
4 egg whites, beaten stiff	Fold in beaten egg whites. Stir batter each time before pouring onto hot greased griddle as rice has a tendency to settle on bottom of mixture.
	Add flavorings such as lemon, peanut butter, banana, rum, coconut or

285

vanilla to batter for a pleasant surprise.

BASIC RICE STUFFING

Preparation and Cooking Time: 30 minutes

Makes about 1 quart, enough to stuff a 6–8 pound bird.

Add your favorite ingredients.

INGREDIENTS
1 medium onion, minced
1 stalk of celery with leaves, chopped
4 tablespoons butter

1 cup uncooked rice

2 cups chicken broth
Salt and freshly ground black pepper to taste
Pinch of sage and/or thyme (optional)

DIRECTIONS
Sauté onion and celery in butter in a skillet over moderate heat until onion is limp and golden.

Add rice and stir-fry until rice becomes transparent.

Add remaining ingredients; cover and cook for 20 minutes or until rice is tender. Adjust seasoning when cooked if necessary. Cool and use as a stuffing.

VARIATIONS
Rice and Mushroom Stuffing. Sauté ½ pound chopped mushrooms along with the onion and celery.

Rice with Raisins and Almonds Stuffing. Omit celery and use 1½ cups beef broth and ½ cup sherry instead of chicken stock, and add half a cup each of raisins and toasted slivered almonds. Season with nutmeg and allspice.

Rice and Chicken Liver Stuffing. Sauté ½ pound chicken livers until browned; remove and mince. Proceed with basic stuffing.

Rice and Sausage stuffing. Cook sausage until browned. Sauté vegetables in fat instead of butter. Proceed with basic stuffing.

BASIC WILD RICE STUFFING

Preparation and Cooking Time: 45 minutes

Makes I quart, enough to stuff a 6–8 pound bird.

Wild rice provides a certain crunch and nuttiness to a stuffing. Use for elegant birds.

INGREDIENTS
1 medium onion, minced
1 stalk of celery with
  leaves, minced

DIRECTIONS
Sauté salt pork until rendered of fat; add onion and celery and cook until

287

¼ cup diced salt pork

onion is limp and golden.

¼ cup minced cooked ham
1 cup wild rice, washed
and drained, or ½ cup
wild rice and ½ cup
brown rice, washed and
drained

Stir-fry ham with vegetables for a moment; then add rice and rosemary and stir-fry to coat.

3 cups chicken broth
Salt and freshly ground
black pepper to taste

Add broth, salt and pepper; cover and bring to a boil. Uncover and boil gently without stirring for 30 minutes until barely tender.
Drain and set on lowest heat to dry for 2–3 minutes, shaking pan now and then. Adjust seasoning if necessary.

VARIATIONS
Add sausage and/or mushrooms.

GREEK RICE STUFFING

Preparation and Cooking Time: 20 minutes

This is the stuffing used in the Greek dish **Arni Yemisto**, a crown roast of lamb or a boned leg of lamb filled with rice, livers, currants and pine nuts.

INGREDIENTS
3 tablespoons butter
¾ cup raw rice

DIRECTIONS
Melt butter in a saucepan; add rice and cook, stirring, until yellow.

1¾ cups hot beef broth

Add broth, cover and cook over low heat for 15 minutes.

3 tablespoons butter
1 cup chopped onions
1 garlic clove, minced
½ pound chicken livers, diced

In a separate skillet, sauté onions, garlic and chicken livers in butter.

⅓ cup currants or raisins
½ cup pine nuts or slivered almonds
¼ cup chopped fresh parsley
2 tablespoons minced fresh mint
Salt and freshly ground black pepper to taste

Mix together rice, sautéed livers, currants, nuts, parsley, mint, and salt and pepper. Taste for seasoning.

INDEX

293

CONDOR
BESTSELLERS

___ **GAMES LAWYERS PLAY WITH YOUR MONEY**
by Blaine N. Simons
(Original Law) $2.25(018-8)

___ **THE GREAT AMERICAN CRAZIES** by James Haskins with
Kathleen Benson and Ellen Inkelis
(Original Sociology) $1.95(014-5)

___ **I AM MARY SHELLEY** by Barbara Lynne Devlin
(Original Occult) $1.95(007-2)

___ **PORTRAITS OF CRIME** by Ector Garcia & Charles E. Pike
(Original Crime) $2.25(010-2)

___ **RHODESIA** by Robin Moore
(Original Non-fiction) $2.25(005-6)

___ **A SURVIVAL KIT FOR A HAPPIER MARRIAGE** by Sam Collins,
Jr., M.D.
(Psychology) $1.75(002-1)

___ **THE WASHINGTON CONNECTION** by Robin Moore,
Lew Perdue with Nick Rowe
(Original Political Science) $2.25(004-8).

At your local bookstore or forward this coupon for
ordering:

Condor Publishing Co., Inc.

Dept MO, 521 Fifth Ave., New York, N.Y. 10017
Please send me the Condor titles I have checked above. Enclosed is
$_____ (please add 50¢ to cover postage and handling). Send
check or money order—no cash or COD's. Order of 5 or more books
postage free.

Name _____

Address _____

City _____ State _____ Zip _____

Please allow at least 4 weeks for delivery.